HARNESS
ASTROLOGY'S
BAD BOY

HARNESS
ASTROLOGY'S
BAD BOY

A HANDBOOK FOR CONQUERING PLUTO'S TUMULTUOUS TRANSIT

Hazel Dixon-Cooper & Bridgett Walther

ATRIA PAPERBACK
New York London Toronto Sydney New Delhi

BEYOND WORDS
Hillsboro, Oregon

ATRIA PAPERBACK

A Division of Simon & Schuster, Inc.
1230 Avenue of the Americas
New York, NY 10020

BEYOND WORDS

20827 N.W. Cornell Road, Suite 500
Hillsboro, Oregon 97124-9808
503-531-8700 / 503-531-8773 fax
www.beyondword.com

Managing editor: Lindsay S. Brown
Editors: Sylvia Spratt, Anna Noak
Copyeditor: Jennifer Weaver-Neist
Proofreader: Michelle Blair
Design: Devon Smith
Composition: William H. Brunson Typography Services

First Atria Paperback/Beyond Words trade paperback edition November 2014

For more information about special discounts for bulk purchases, please contact Simon & Schuster Special Sales at 1-866-506-1949 or business@simonandschuster.com.

The Simon & Schuster Speakers Bureau can bring authors to your live event. For more information or to book an event, contact the Simon & Schuster Speakers Bureau at 1-866-248-3049 or visit our website at www.simonspeakers.com.

Manufactured in the United States of America

10 9 8 7 6 5 4 3 2 1

Library of Congress Cataloging-in-Progress Data

Dixon-Cooper, Hazel,
    Harness astrology's bad boy : a handbook for conquering Pluto's tumultuous transit : / Hazel Dixon-Cooper and Bridgett Walther.—First Atria Paperback/Beyond Words trade paperback edition.
        pages   cm
    1. Pluto (D warf planet)--Miscellanea. 2. Astrology. I. Title.
    BF1724.2.P4D59 2014
    133.5'392—dc23   2014023000

ISBN 978-1-58270-455-5
ISBN 978-1-4767-3549-8 (eBook)

The corporate mission of Beyond Words Publishing, Inc.: *Inspire to Integrity*

For Bonnie Hearn Hill and Christopher Allan Poe,
two Pluto-inspired souls who never met
a challenge they didn't like.
—Hazel Dixon-Cooper

To my very patient husband, David,
for his determination and understanding.
—Bridgett Walther

CONTENTS

Why We Wrote This Book   ix

Introduction   xi

    Who Is Pluto?   xiv

    Five Ways to Gain and Grow with Pluto   xv

Part One: Pluto Through the Generations

Pluto in Aries   2

Pluto in Taurus   4

Pluto in Gemini   4

Pluto in Cancer   5

Pluto in Leo   6

Pluto in Virgo   7

Pluto in Libra   8

Pluto in Scorpio   9

Pluto in Sagittarius   10

Pluto in Capricorn   11

Pluto in Aquarius   11

Pluto in Pisces   12

Part Two: The Sun Signs

Aries (March 21–April 19)   17

Taurus (April 20–May 20)   21

Gemini (May 21–June 20)   26

Cancer (June 21–July 22)   30

Leo (July 23–August 22)   35

Virgo (August 23–September 22)   39

Libra (September 23–October 22)   43

Scorpio (October 23–November 21)   48

Sagittarius (November 22–December 21)   53

Capricorn (December 22–January 19)   57

Aquarius (January 20–February 18)   61
Pisces (February 19–March 20)   66

Part Three: Pluto and the Houses

Pluto in the First House: The Phoenix of Identity   81
Pluto in the Second House: The Phoenix of Values   93
Pluto in the Third House: The Phoenix of Truth   103
Pluto in the Fourth House: The Phoenix of Nurturing   115
Pluto in the Fifth House: The Phoenix of Creativity   125
Pluto in the Sixth House: The Phoenix of Service   135
Pluto in the Seventh House: The Phoenix of Partnership   145
Pluto in the Eighth House: The Phoenix of Legacy   155
Pluto in the Ninth House: The Phoenix of Belief   165
Pluto in the Tenth House: The Phoenix of Integrity   173
Pluto in the Eleventh House: The Phoenix of Revolution   185
Pluto in the Twelfth House: The Phoenix of Acceptance   197

Conclusion: Conquering Your World with Pluto   207
Acknowledgments   211
Resources and Recommended Reading   213
Quick Guide to Roman Gods and Other Mythological
    People and Creatures   215
Glossary   217

WHY WE WROTE THIS BOOK

Ever since the first person scratched a picture into the rocks of a cave, humans have studied the stars. For thousands of years, astrologers have used the stars to forecast events, identify medical conditions, give self-help advice, and more.

Astrology is a practice that few confess to believing in but one that millions use. Who doesn't check a horoscope in the paper now and again? Many people still swear by the Moon-based advice in the *Farmers' Almanac*. Today, astrology is often used as a supplemental guiding force that helps people everywhere—celebrities, to professionals, to us average folks—better understand both the world and ourselves.

Many people desperately seek ways to heal the emotional holes in their lives through a variety of techniques both ancient and modern. As professional astrologers, we've dedicated our lives to helping people through this ancient system of self-knowledge, and we consult with people from all walks of life on a daily basis. In the ongoing service of this mission, we've created this in-depth guide to gaining insight into the problematic areas of life and, from that insight, pathways that lead toward a more fulfilled existence.

In this book, we concentrated on Pluto, the planet of destruction and transformation. You may have read that, in 2006, Pluto was downgraded to a "dwarf" planet by the International Astronomical Union. Simply put, astronomy is the science of mapping the sky and tracking the movement of all the objects within the known universe. Astrology is the practice of interpreting the movement of the planets in our solar system as it relates to human behavior. Just as with everything else, size doesn't matter, especially with the badass of the universe. Whether some humans call Pluto a planet, a dwarf, or a rock in space, his influence and purpose in astrology hasn't changed. Pluto is still the force of transformation, the tough guy, astrology's hard case. And astrology uses "planet" as a reference to the farthest rock from the Sun. In our work, and this book, so do we.

Pluto deals with what is buried or hidden in the psyche. Conditioned behaviors, unresolved fears, and anger are some of the issues this astrological bad boy raises, as Pluto's energy works through the self-destructive scenarios we repeat that cause us pain. These issues are revealed through the house placements of Pluto, both by birth and during a transit through the astrology chart. Wherever Pluto appears, it illustrates lifelong challenges and opportunities.

Throughout this book, we have integrated examples taken from our real-life files, although names, occupations, and other descriptive information have been changed to protect the privacy of our clients. Our intent is to show you how to recognize the harmful emotional or physical patterns that you subconsciously repeat so that you can break free of self-defeating behaviors and use Pluto's influence as a force for positive change in your life.

We've seen Pluto's work in our own lives. We've felt the flow of Pluto's energy. When we ignored it, we got our butts kicked, just like you probably have. But when we harnessed Pluto's strength as a force of change instead of destruction, we found a way out of our inner turmoil and a path toward a better, brighter future. The choice is yours.

INTRODUCTION

A friend seems to thrive no matter what life throws at her while you feel like you're stuck on that endless hamster wheel. Maybe you feel like a loser-magnet when it comes to finding a lover or you can't find a satisfying job. Perhaps you're afraid to stand up for yourself or you're rebelling in self-destructive ways. Why?

The simple truth is that you are probably the reason you're stuck like a rodent in a cage. But hey, don't feel bad. You're not alone. Most of us humans have to learn our lessons the hard way. Sometimes, it takes the emotional equivalent of being hit by an eighteen-wheeler before we recognize our role in attracting those unhealthy situations that we can't seem to avoid. You could spend thousands of dollars and months or years in therapy. You could read every self-help book on the market. You could have your horoscope mapped and charted and analyzed by a dozen astrologers. But until you decide to change, nothing will work.

In order to transform, the first step forward is to become aware of the negative patterns you keep repeating. Then you must make a conscious decision to change. How do you achieve such a transformation? By becoming mindful of the automatic responses and misconceptions about yourself that you learned in childhood and then continued to perpetuate throughout your adult life. Seem impossible? It isn't.

One of the easiest ways to learn about these ingrained patterns is through astrology. It's the original self-help tool that contains every key you need to live a fulfilling life. It's been said that astrology is the first psychology. Five thousand years before Sigmund Freud developed his theory of psychoanalysis, astrologers had learned to correlate planetary movements with both personality and behavior patterns. As a self-help tool, it provides amazing insight into the underlying character traits that can either impede or propel your spiritual and psychological growth.

Carl Jung was a Swiss psychologist and psychiatrist who is considered by many to be the founder of analytic psychology. Jung was Freud's protégé and friend, and he also had a deep interest in astrology. Jung cast the horoscopes of his patients and made a statistical study of the relationships of marriage partners. He recognized that astrology could be used as an important tool for self-awareness. In a September 9, 1947, letter to B. V. Raman, one of the most respected astrologers in the world (reproduced in Roderick Main's *Jung On Synchronicity and the Paranormal*, Princeton University Press, 1998), Jung wrote, "In cases of difficult psychological diagnosis, I usually get a horoscope in order to have a further point of view from an entirely different angle. I must say that I very often found that the astrological data elucidated certain points which I otherwise would have been unable to understand."

Today, many psychologists and psychiatrists are also accomplished astrologers, and countless others regularly consult with astrologers in order to gain greater insight into their clients.

Since Babylonian times, this ancient practice has been used to guide people by interpreting the movement of the planets in our solar system as it relates to human behavior. In fact, every civilization has a form of astrology designed to help us find inner happiness and live vital lives. And just as every ancient civilization looked to the stars for answers, we modern human beings would be wise to do the same, recognizing that we are all part of the universe, and are subject to its rhythms and cycles just as the tides are influenced by the Moon. We contain the same physical elements that compose the Earth and share the same human ability to reason that sets us apart from all other living things—and yet we are as unique as the stars. Your personal natal chart is a snapshot of where the planets were the minute you were born. No one, not even your twin, is exactly like you.

Each of the planets in the zodiac has a specific role in shaping the inner you, but none is more important or makes a bigger impact than Pluto, the planet of destruction and transformation. In mythology, Pluto, the god, exposes the shadows of the past that can paralyze the present and destroy the future; and the discovery of the planet that carries his name coincides with the beginnings of psychoanalysis. Like a good-but-tough therapist, astrology's Pluto tries to wring the truth out of you. His job is to challenge you to live an honest and fearless life. Your job is to deal with the truths that prevent your happiness.

Before we go any further, you need to know that no one's Pluto journey is easy. The world is flooded with quick-fix guides, workshops, and therapies to find success, love, and happiness. But where Pluto is concerned, you quickly learn that there is no quick fix, and the meaning of self-help is just that—you must help yourself. You must be willing to do the annoying, sometimes hurtful, sometimes bitter, but in the end always rewarding work.

Pluto is an in-your-face guy, and we've loaded the book with in-your-face advice. Sometimes that advice will be edgy, sometimes dark, but it will always be accompanied by humor. With this in mind, know that our intention is first and foremost to use Pluto to teach you how to overcome some of your most difficult and ingrained traits to clear the path to positive self-realization and transformation.

Although you might not realize it, you have an inner light and spiritual love that will support and sustain you through turmoil. You inherited this power the moment you were born. With this book, you're going to learn how to unlock the heroic part of your soul to allow yourself to flourish as you were intended. Nothing in astrology is predestined. There's no mysterious secret to making it work for you. Life's difficulties may feel like fate, but you hold the key to your transformation. The choice of how you will live is yours. Once you choose positive change, you can begin to walk through life in awareness.

Pluto's reputation is a scary one because he rules death. But the death associated with him is the death of your self-destructive behaviors. He also rules buried riches, both within the Earth and within you. His most powerful symbol is the phoenix, the magical bird that was reborn again and again from its own ashes. No matter what life throws at the phoenix, it can't be destroyed. It always triumphs. So can you. This book will show you how.

Who Is Pluto?

Before we jump into Pluto's story, it will be helpful for you to know that the names of the planets in our Western Astrology are based on Roman mythology, which is heavily blended with Greek mythology. In a nutshell, the Romans took the Greek gods, changed most of their names, kept some of the Greek myths, and added their own twist to other ancient stories.

As you'll see below, and in the Sun Signs section, the Greek names are presented in parentheses throughout the book. For further reference, you'll find the helpful table, Quick Guide to Roman Gods and Other Mythological People and Creatures (page 215).

Now who is this character and why is he such a bad boy? In Roman mythology, Pluto was the lord of the underworld. He ruled Hades (also the Greek name for him) and all the hidden realms of Earth—everything that's dead, buried, or deliberately concealed belongs to him. He's the expert on power plays, control freaks, and hidden agendas because he was born into the poster family for dysfunction.

Pluto, Neptune (Poseidon), and Jupiter (Zeus) were the sons of Saturn (Cronus) and Ops (Rhea). Saturn was the head of the Titans, a gang of ruthless gods who ruled everything in the sky, on the Earth, and below the Earth. Saturn, a mean paranoid who killed his own father in a takeover, set himself up as Supreme Ruler. Think of a mob war with Tony Soprano surviving as boss badass—only, Saturn wasn't as nice as Tony. When Saturn's sons were born, he was so fearful of falling victim to the same fate he had dealt his old man that he swallowed each of them—or so he thought. Ops managed to save Jupiter by handing Saturn a swaddled rock and hiding the baby on the island of Crete.

When Jupiter grew up, he caught up with Saturn and forced him to cough up his brothers. Together, they led their gang, the Olympians, in a ten-year war against Saturn and the Titans. Keeping the family tradition alive—and fulfilling their father's worst fear—Jupiter killed Saturn. Then the three boys drew straws for his kingdom. Jupiter won the sky and the title of Supreme Ruler. Neptune won the sea. Pluto got what was left—Hades, the Land of the Dead. He rules secrets, obsession, jealousy, and revenge. And wherever he operates, he moves behind the scenes.

Today, think of him as astrology's version of the Godfather. He's the mob boss who doesn't care whether you're the most pious person on the block or the adulterer next door. He makes you the offer you can't refuse. Revise that. You have free will to choose, but you *shouldn't* refuse. Work with his tough-guy energy, and you'll find the courage to stand up to anything and to transform your life.

Saturn, the planet of karma, rules Capricorn. Pluto, the planet of transformation, is also considered a planet of fate. Each deals with areas in which you need to do some work in order to evolve. The years these two powerhouses travel together through your personal horoscope bring situations that can definitely feel like the universe is kicking you. However, you can have decades to make permanent changes because the process is extremely slow. Pluto spends from twelve to thirty years in a zodiac sign and in the one or two houses it occupies in your natal chart during a transit. He works through time and pressure—the same principle of time and pressure that it takes to create the buried riches within the Earth.

Five Ways to Gain and Grow with Pluto

This book is designed to help you to understand how Pluto works in your life, and to use that understanding to enact positive change. Pluto's mission as he moves through your natal chart is to make you recognize the negative patterns that prevent you from realizing your full potential.

The zodiac wheel is a pie chart divided into twelve equal segments called houses, and each house is home to one of the Sun signs. Each house also represents specific life areas and symbolizes the soul's journey around the zodiac. The five significant areas of Pluto's personal influence on you are your Sun sign, your Ascendant (rising sign), the house Pluto occupies in your natal chart, the house Pluto is currently transiting, and, to a lesser extent, your Pluto generation.

Imagine you're looking at Pluto through a high-powered telescope set to capture a wide-angle view of the universe. At this angle, Pluto looks like a dot in the middle of a huge amount of space, but you do see him. This is what viewing Pluto's influence on your generation is like. You share certain collective traits such as fashion trends or perhaps being particularly technology savvy, and you feel Pluto's presence through the political and societal changes that molded the world during your growing years.

Next, flip the focus to a closer view, where Pluto is clearly visible and a lot bigger in the frame. This picture represents the influence on your Sun and rising signs. Pluto's effect on your life is stronger here, and you feel the pressure he exerts in a more personal way.

Finally, switch to close-up, and Pluto's right in your face. You feel as if you could reach out and touch him, and that he could definitely reach out and whack you. This is what it looks like when Pluto's force is concentrated in your natal house, and through the houses he transits during your lifetime. This angle is the up-close-and-personal shot, and there's no way to avoid looking directly into Pluto's penetrating stare.

Reading the section "Pluto Through the Generations" (part one) will provide you with a more global view of how each generation is affected by Pluto's presence. And the sections about your Sun sign, rising sign, natal Pluto, and transiting Pluto (parts two and three) will give you an in-depth and unique look at the ways in which this powerful energy is working in your life.

Natal Chart

So, what exactly is a natal chart? Imagine a photograph taken mere moments after a baby is born, captured perhaps by a proud father or helpful delivery-room nurse. Your personal natal chart is like that—it's an astrological snapshot of where the planets were located in the sky at the moment you were born and is exclusive to you alone.

Your natal chart is your personal zodiac wheel, and having a copy of your natal chart handy will help enormously as you make your way through the chapters ahead. You can easily obtain a copy of your natal chart through a number of online sources. And please visit either Hazel's or Bridgett's website (located in the Resources and Recommended Reading section at the end of this book) to reach out to either of us with questions about your natal chart.

Pluto Through the Generations

A detailed table of the years Pluto was in each Sun sign is located in part one of this book. This will help you determine to which Pluto generation you belong. Then each section that follows contains a brief discussion of how Pluto got his hooks into that generation, showing the collective mindset as well as some of the changes that occurred during Pluto's visit. We also take a humorous look at what humanity might expect from future Pluto generations.

Sun Signs and Ascendants (Rising Signs)

Part two will take you on a journey through your Sun sign and some of the general ways in which Pluto's transit can affect you. The respective Sun sign information also provides insight into your Ascendant, further deepening Pluto's unrelenting influence. For example, if you are an Aquarius with Libra rising, read both the Aquarius and Libra Sun sign sections.

Until 2024, Pluto will be traveling through the astrological sign of Capricorn. The last time he elbowed his way into this tradition-loving space was from 1762 to 1778. A game-changing event during this time was the American Revolution, when rebels fought for their independence and freedom from a power they believed to be oppressive and unjust. The American revolutionaries struggled against control, greed, and unchecked power. Today, these themes are playing out globally in widespread battles for freedom, across many cultures and countries.

Capricorn is the Cardinal Earth sign that represents authority and power structures—governments, armies, corporations, and bureaucracies. Cardinal signs take action, sometimes disregarding the consequences. (The Cardinal Quality and the Capricorn Sun sign are discussed further in part two.) The tenth house, Capricorn's home, signifies career and public life. Some of the issues in the tenth house include ambition, greed, and domination. Upheavals occur when we rebel—either individually or collectively—against the power figures in our lives. Pluto's purpose is to destroy anything that prevents the soul's evolution or inhibits freedom.

Think of it this way. Capricorn wants to be absolute ruler, no questions asked. Pluto makes it his business to strip away the facade of false security to expose the behind-the-scenes lies and corruption of power. When Pluto and Capricorn team up, you'd better strap in and hang on.

Since Pluto moved into Capricorn in 2008, we've seen revolutions spring up all over the world as people fight for more personal freedoms. We've witnessed economic downturns caused by unchecked corporate greed. We've seen how putting money and power before human rights has led to a worldwide financial crisis. Even the planet itself is endangered by global warming, water and air pollution, and a rise in drug-resistant diseases.

On a personal level, wherever this Pluto-Capricorn battle is affecting your Sun sign and rising sign will reveal possible areas in which you may be struggling with authority and rigid rules of conduct that you've accepted as normal behavior. In short, Pluto exists to stir the pot, and the Pluto-Capricorn brawl knocks the pot off the stove then goes right ahead and starts a kitchen fire.

Houses

In part three of this book, the focus sharpens as the details of both your natal house and the house through which Pluto's transiting are examined. Suppose Pluto's moving through your First House of Self. Hello, identity crisis! If you were born with Pluto in the first house, you may have struggled with identity issues throughout your life. In the Seventh House of Partnership, you could face control and manipulation concerns within your close relationships. A trip through (or natal Pluto in) your Fourth House of Home and Family might find you rebelling against family tradition. Suddenly, you have the urge to ruin your mom's expectations for you to marry that nice accountant by running away on a cross-country road trip with a guy from the local Harley club instead. Maybe you choose a quiet homebody your tatted-up relatives think is boring. You get the idea.

Each house contains several themes that are explained in the individual house sections, and you could experience Pluto upheavals in one or more of these areas. Your hardest work begins within the houses because these areas are Pluto's specific targets as he yanks all of the skeletons out of your life's closet. And as you read about these houses, ask yourself to name some of the absolutes you were taught to believe—either about yourself, your family, or the world—in relation to the areas ruled by that particular house. How do they affect you today? Do you still conform to the family propaganda? If so, in what way? Questioning ingrained patterns is one of the first steps on the path to your Pluto transformation.

Becoming Mindful

As you read the ways in which Pluto's energy can affect your life, if a theme or issue strikes a nerve, pause for a moment to think about why you may feel a particular emotion. If a negative behavior that's brought up in the text is also one of your habits, try to pinpoint where you learned it and why. Is it a protective measure? Is it a family trait that you automatically assumed? The same goes for stories about real-world people that are used as examples throughout this book. How do you identify with them? Can you think of the reason or the event in your own life that connects you to a certain story?

Being mindful is nothing more than the habit of thinking about what you're doing. Do you reach for food when you're not hungry? What are you really hungry for? Do you nod in agreement like a bobble-head doll even though you might not agree? Why are you reluctant to speak your mind?

This is a long, gradual process, and that's the way it's supposed to be. The first step is to slow down and think about what you do, so that you can begin to recognize the auto-responses and self-defense mechanisms that are preventing your emotional or spiritual growth.

Pluto is the force that exerts the steady, nagging pressure in your head that something in your life needs to change. When Pluto knocks on your door, he comes armed with a list of truths that you probably won't want to face. You can go into fight-or-flight mode, but neither one works with this tough guy. If you run, he'll catch up with you in the form of yet another painful experience sooner or later. Try to fight him by refusing to help yourself and you'll simply remain stuck in neutral, spinning your wheels, going nowhere.

Or you can take a stand. You can tackle the challenges Pluto churns up. Yes, he's the big bad boy of the universe, but Pluto's only a real bully if you let him be. Be mindful of your choices, your actions, and most of all, the way you handle the punches he throws your way, and you'll discover that you can transform any negative pattern into a force for your spiritual growth.

PART ONE

Pluto Through the Generations

Pluto spends approximately twelve to thirty years in each sign. These long transits characterize the generations by influencing the cultural obsessions and lifelong fascinations of the people born during those years.

Remember the telescope lens and the wide-angle view of the sky? In this section, we're looking at the big picture of Pluto situated right out on the edge of the universe. Your generational Pluto helps explain some of the core belief systems and cultural trends shared by everyone born during Pluto's transit through a particular sign. It's another layer in understanding the forces that shaped your character. Just as Pluto pushes you personally to grow and change, he pushes each generation to search out and eliminate the destructive issues handed down to them from their predecessors. Heard of the generation gap? Pluto is the force that drives each group to evolve beyond and do better than their parents.

Each Pluto generation has two main themes. The first is how the people born in the generation shove the undercurrents or issues to the surface (basically, all that stuff that their parents didn't want to face). The second shows how the generation looks at and changes the world for the better (or the worse) as they grow up. It can also be useful (and fun too) to look toward the future for Pluto generations, speculating on what's next as Pluto continues to stir the cosmic pot for generations to come.

Something to note before we jump in—a Pluto generation timeframe is usually longer that what is commonly referred to as a "generation." For example, although the majority of Baby Boomers belong to the Pluto-in-Leo generation, not all were born during that transit. The Baby Boomer generation's birth dates cover 1946 to 1964, and Pluto's transit of Leo was from 1937 to 1956. That's why it's important to find your personal Pluto generation in the table below.

Pluto Table

Find your birth date below to determine to which Pluto generation you belong. If your birthday falls in one of Pluto's retrograde periods (the shaded boxes), read both the sign it was in when you were born and the sign preceding it. For example, if you were born on March 10, 1939, when Pluto was retrograde in Cancer for a few months, read the Cancer and Leo sections because you will have traits of both the Leo and Cancer generations.

Pluto in Aries (1823–1852) and (2066–2095)

In America, this hardy generation of the past was born on wagon trains and in frontier settlements. Their parents were pioneers who pushed west one step ahead of civilization. Pluto's strong will fueled Aries's determination to succeed, and the generation born during this transit capitalized on that independent spirit by furthering the Industrial Revolution that began in Great Britain and expanding it well into the 1900s.

Around the world, independence was the battle cry as disruptive Pluto moved through fearless and volatile Aries. Belgium won its independence from the Netherlands. The Greeks gained their freedom from Turkish rule. Hungary declared its independence from the Austrian Empire.

Pluto-in-Aries of the future will no doubt establish the first colony on Mars, and then, true to their pioneering spirit, use the outpost as a base from which to explore the planets. Perhaps they'll clone the first universal soldier army. These characters will no doubt spend half their lifetimes reversing the peace-promoting laws of the Pisces-Pluto generation that precedes them.

Dates	Pluto Generation	Dates	Pluto Generation	Dates	Pluto Generation	Dates	Pluto Generation	Dates	Pluto Generation
May 26, 1914 to Oct. 6, 1937	♋ CANCER	Jan. 14, 1957 to Aug. 17, 1957	♌ LEO	Nov. 5, 1983 to May 17, 1984	♏ SCORPIO	June 13, 2008 to Nov. 25, 2008	♐ SAGITTARIUS	Mar. 8, 2043 to Aug. 30, 2043	♓ PISCES
Oct. 7, 1937 to Nov. 24, 1937	♌ LEO	Aug. 18, 1957 to Apr. 10, 1958	♍ VIRGO	May 18, 1984 to Aug. 27, 1984	♎ LIBRA	Nov. 26, 2008 to Mar. 22, 2023	♑ CAPRICORN	Aug. 31, 2043 to Jan. 18, 2044	♒ AQUARIUS
Nov. 25, 1937 to Aug. 2, 1938	♋ CANCER	Apr. 11, 1958 to June 9, 1958	♌ LEO	Aug. 28, 1984 to Jan. 16, 1995	♏ SCORPIO	Mar. 23, 2023 to June 9, 2023	♒ AQUARIUS	Jan. 19, 2044 to June 17, 2066	♓ PISCES
Aug. 3, 1938 to Feb. 6, 1939	♌ LEO	June 10, 1958 to Oct. 4, 1971	♍ VIRGO	Jan. 17, 1995 to Apr. 19, 1995	♐ SAGITTARIUS	June 10, 2023 to Jan. 19, 2024	♑ CAPRICORN	June 18, 2066 to July 9, 2066	♈ ARIES
Feb. 7, 1939 to June 12, 1939	♋ CANCER	Oct. 5, 1971 to Apr. 16, 1972	♎ LIBRA	Apr. 20, 1995 to Nov. 9, 1995	♏ SCORPIO	Jan. 20, 2024 to Aug. 31, 2024	♒ AQUARIUS	July 10, 2066 to Apr. 7, 2067	♓ PISCES
June 13, 1939 to Oct. 19, 1956	♌ LEO	Apr. 17, 1972 to July 29, 1972	♍ VIRGO	Nov. 10, 1995 to Jan. 24, 2008	♐ SAGITTARIUS	Sept. 1, 2024 to Nov. 18, 2024	♑ CAPRICORN	Apr. 8, 2067 to Sept. 26, 2067	♈ ARIES
Oct. 20, 1956 to Jan. 13, 1957	♍ VIRGO	July 30, 1972 to Nov. 4, 1983	♎ LIBRA	Jan. 25, 2008 to June 12, 2008	♑ CAPRICORN	Nov. 19, 2024 to Mar. 7, 2043	♒ AQUARIUS	Sept. 27, 2067 to Feb. 22, 2068	♓ PISCES

Pluto in Taurus (1853–1883) and (2095–2127)

When Pluto, the planet of obsession and transformation, connected with Taurus, the sign of possessions and stability, the result produced a past generation that was preoccupied with making money and keeping it. They added assembly lines to speed product output, and crisscrossed the continent with railroad tracks to ship their goods in record time, ensuring they made as much cash as they could as fast as possible.

A significant social upheaval during this time was the American Civil War. Taurus is the sign of ownership; and although it is peace loving, Taurus equates possessions with security and dislikes change. Pluto tears down anything that prevents the soul's evolution; so when he moved into this possessive space, he stirred up the social conscience of that part of the Pluto-in-Aries group that demanded freedom and independence for everyone.

Worldwide, Japan allowed trade with America, Russia sold natural resource-rich Alaska to the U.S., and the French captured rich Mexico City during Pluto's tour of financially focused Taurus.

Pluto-in-Taurus of the future will pick up the pieces of the future Pluto-Aries obsession with war and destruction, and lay groundwork to rebuild financial and environmental systems. When we finally get going on those colonies on Mars, the future Pluto-in-Taurus generation will probably be the ones controlling the supply chains that keep the Martian colonies alive.

Pluto in Gemini (1884–1914) and (2127–2157)

Popularized by Ernest Hemingway as the "Lost Generation" in his book *The Sun Also Rises*, most of these men and women reached adulthood during World War I. Although many seemed to inherit Gemini's cynical view of life and general aimlessness, this group was (and will be) both intellectual and progressive on the whole.

Pluto-in-Gemini kids grew up pioneering the phonograph, telephone, and electric light. They brought global communications to an unheard of level of sophistication through their inventions of television, radio, and the telephone. These multitasking dynamos capitalized on the energy of the Taurus-Pluto oil barons and added a spider web of roads across the United States to accommodate the mass production of automobiles.

Examples of this generation's intellectual enlightenment include New Zealand becoming the first country to allow women to vote, and the establishment of the Nobel Prizes for Peace, Science, and Literature. Albert Einstein announced his Theory of Relativity and Sigmund Freud published his *Interpretation of Dreams*.

The Pluto-in-Gemini generation also created the movie magazines of the fifties—precursors to today's gossip rags and social networks.

True to their love of all things new and techy, future Pluto-in-Gemini people will find even faster ways to communicate, perhaps through brain implants that allow instant access to everything.

Pluto in Cancer (1914–1939)

Called "the Greatest Generation" by journalist and author Tom Brokaw in his book of the same title, this generation was born when the world was on the brink of disaster. World War I and the Great Depression affected their birth and childhood, and they grew up obsessed with creating and maintaining the ideal home.

Ever heard of "the hostess with the mostess"? Hospitality was one of the hallmarks of the Pluto-in-Cancer generation, and so was protecting the family image. The Cancer generation perfected the cover-up—think of all those fifties TV shows where perfect families lived perfect lives in perfectly safe worlds. However, beneath the fantasy, the double standard raged.

On the other side of this coin, some Pluto-in-Cancer babies cleared the way for the Beat Generation of the fifties. The term "beat" meant that this group of rebels were tired or beat down, but "beat" also came to mean upbeat and even beatific, drawing parallels to this generation's unquenchable thirst for life despite the early odds stacked against them.

Globally, paranoia played out during this time through an escalating arms race. Protection was this generation's driving force, and they finally invented the A-bomb to guarantee it. However, this my-gun-is-bigger-than-yours mentality brought it to the brink of World War II and the further escalation of international espionage. During the fifties, the communism scare resulted in the McCarthy hearings and the Hollywood blacklist, both of which are classic examples of Cancer-Pluto paranoia taken to the extreme.

Ultimately, self-sacrifice to protect the home and family was this group's goal. Even when it backfired, their intentions were always noble. Thanks to the Cancer-Plutos' desire to care for others, welfare was created in the hope that people would always have access to the basic necessities of life.

Today, this generation is experiencing the effects of Pluto in Capricorn within some of their closest relationships. As they reflect on their lives to date, Pluto asks them to heal their personal wounds of the past and to strengthen their bonds with family, friends, and others they're close to. They still have much to offer in the way of teaching the world about returning to past values of self-sacrifice for the common good.

Pluto in Leo (1937–1956)

Cancer moves behind the scenes, but Leo thrives in the spotlight. The Pluto-in-Leo generation is best known as the Baby Boomers or, as Thomas Wolfe labeled them in the 1970s, the "Me Generation."

The sheer numbers of these kids ensured that marketing campaigns were targeted at what they wanted. And the Leo Sun sign is theatrical. This bunch grew up thinking that the world revolved around them, and the generation gap between the Leo-Plutos and their Cancer-Pluto predecessors is one of the largest in history.

Cancer-Plutos often sacrificed themselves for the sake of family. They invented the plastic smile and the "everything's fine" plastic truth as they covered up for drunken relatives and holiday brawls. In contrast, Leo-Plutos threw the family skeletons on center stage for the world to see. As hippies, they believed in putting sex, drugs, and rock and roll on display, and they dared anyone, including their hand-wringing parents, to stop them.

It's no astrological surprise that both Valium and the birth control pill hit the market in 1960 as Pluto-in-Leo disrupted the patriarchy and influenced women of all ages to rebel against the traditional roles of wife and mother. Women refused to be boxed in by a society that wanted to keep them as second-class citizens.

This group is also a study in contradictions. Many turned to drugs and uninhibited sex, away from traditional gender and societal roles. Many more marched on Washington, fighting for equality. They lobbied for peace, helping to end the Vietnam War, and refueled the women's movement started by their great-grandmothers.

"Sixty is the new thirty" is their current battle cry. These wild children refuse to age, turning fitness, face-and-body-altering procedures, and live-forever diets into multibillion-dollar industries.

Pluto's transit through Capricorn affects the Leo generation in the area of service to others and everyday work. As young adults, the Leos were activists for social change Today, this still-dynamic group continues to help stoke the fires of global equality—in their usual flamboyant way, of course.

Pluto in Virgo (1956–1971)

As flower children who pushed the hippie movement through the middle 1970s, some of the early-born Pluto-Virgo babies were often lumped together as dirty, lazy, drug-addled freeloaders who couldn't be bothered to get off the couch and get a job—but they also turned Virgo idealism into a vision of communal life and love.

Later-born Pluto-Virgos were the first wave of Generation X, and unlike their Leo-Pluto parents, they actually thrived on stability. These kids perfected the advertising systems that sell the Baby Boomers every antiaging solution and diet scam on the market. They're the cubicle dwellers who thrive on crunching numbers and developing precise systems of checks and balances. They represent the silent majority who, like a colony of ants, has the power to desiccate the carcass of big business and political corruption all over the world.

Surprises of any kind give Virgo-Plutos hives. They strive for balance between abject materialism and saving the Earth by driving hybrid vehicles and wearing secondhand clothes. We owe large-scale organic farming and recycling programs to this generation.

Amazing advancements in both traditional and preventive medicine are the result of this group's devotion to health. They fight to repair the national healthcare system, and have brought alternative medicine into the mainstream via the corner vitamin shop and supermarket health-food section.

Collectively, this generation feels their input is invaluable to the world. They pretend to have all the answers because they've perfected the art of cherry-picking statistics and twisting information to support their point of view. These pollsters and survey takers were born with a con artist's talent for double-dealing.

As Pluto-in-Capricorn transits their life area of creativity and drama, "get real" is the war cry they fire at the still far-left, far-right, or just far-out Leo-Pluto bunch. However, Pluto's challenge to the Virgo-Pluto generation is to lighten up and remember that nobody's perfect.

Pluto in Libra (1971–1983)

The majority of Gen-Xers are Pluto-Libras. They're also called the "MTV Generation," and although they grew up pushing the boundaries on everything from music to culture to politics to sexuality, they ultimately seek equality and balance in their world. They're also relationship junkies who crave romance, inventing metrosexual culture, speed dating, and online matchmaking. They're tolerant, too, and have pushed hard for human rights and social diversity.

Libra-Plutos believe in social justice and work hard against discrimination in any form. This is the peacekeeper group who would like to teach the world how to live in harmony. They seek fair relationships in every way, and many of them have chosen human rights as their life's work.

Pluto in Capricorn is testing Libra-Pluto's tolerance in the area of home and family. They're being asked to apply the same fair-minded, nonprejudiced concern they have for the world to their family. And to also consider what home and family truly means to them.

Pluto in Scorpio (1982–1995)

Pluto rules Scorpio, and these two were made for each other. Ghosts, death, an IRS audit—nothing frightens the Pluto-in-Scorpio generation. The first of the Millennials, this wild bunch is full of conspiracy theorists, activists, and the ultimate tellers of tall tales—which they incessantly tweet, post, and text about.

In high school, they wrapped themselves in chains and head-to-toe black in true Goth style. Today, they love to frighten older generations with news of the latest rogue virus or widening hole in the ozone. Despite their tough persona, however, this group is very close to their parents. And although they thrive on their radical image, Pluto-in-Scorpios have their share of contradictions as well. For example, they're very committed to saving the environment—as long as it doesn't interfere with owning a rebuilt muscle car or a three-miles-to-the-gallon SUV.

Like their Gen-X older cousins, Scorpio-Plutos are stuck with the aftermath of the free-love era. Sex appeals to them, but the growing global awareness of the devastation of AIDS and other sexual health topics during their youth took the fun out of it—almost. Excelling in the fields of medicine, scientific research, and government reform, this group will root out the causes of decay and discover cures that transform. They might take cloning to the next level of grow-your-own replacement body parts, discover a cure for cancer, or even figure out a way to make us live forever.

Whatever their future holds, Scorpio-Plutos were born into a world with huge problems that threaten to spiral out of control. As a whole, this generation is serious and committed to whatever they do. They've appeared on Earth at just the right moment to save the human race with their fearless courage.

Pluto in Capricorn is circulating through this generation's communication area, challenging them to speak up and take a stand against any tradition that threatens either the individual or the planet. This generation can change the world for the better if they unite for the common good.

Pluto in Sagittarius (1995–2008)

Enter Generation Y, also Millennials, only lightened up to the point of being a little spacy. Born with a smartphone in one hand and a laptop in the other, these kids are too busy connecting with their new friends in the Amazon rainforest to listen to what you have to say. They believe in absolute social freedom for every soul on Earth. To them, organized religion is passé because they're plugged into the universal spirit. At least that's the excuse they give when they drop out of Sunday school to form their own alternative religion.

This generation has some serious attention-span issues. They alternate between rushing everywhere at once and sleeping for twenty-four hours straight. They are the ultimate "more is better / biggest is best" generation. They know no boundaries, and embrace the world as both their oyster and their classroom. They're a hopeful lot, and sometimes cheerful to the point of being clownish.

Living under the shadows of the terrorist attacks of September 11, 2001, and the subsequent ripples in politics, warfare, and international terrorism will only fuel their optimism that humans can reconcile their differences. Through their love of knowledge, this generation can open dialogues that truly get somewhere. They will rejuvenate education and law, and might even prove to be the first generation in history to actually help the rest of us learn *from* history.

In the meantime, these kids need freedom to investigate the world without prejudice, because Sagittarius-Plutos hold no malice in their souls. Give them room to roam and grow within sensible rather than fear-based guidelines.

Pluto-in-Capricorn dares Sagittarius-Plutos to rethink their personal value systems and to question the existing value systems of the world. This generation has the power to redirect the force of human destiny through the breaking down of the religious and cultural barriers that separate mankind, and Pluto-in-Capricorn is just the kick in the butt they need to do so. They will find themselves challenged throughout their lives to pay attention to the world and take part in it, not just sit on it.

Pluto in Capricorn (2008–2023)

These babies are born flipping off the world as Pluto pushes the obstinate quality of Capricorn into a total obsession for control. From the time they first wail hello, they do not tolerate traditional rules. These are the kids whose first-grade essay will be a petition to oust a teacher they dislike.

Starting with the schoolyard bullies and ending with human-rights oppressors, Capricorn-Plutos will hold the world accountable for its crap. This generation won't tolerate the abuse of power in any form—but especially against the helpless. As adults, they will have the power to become the voice of the voiceless. They are the revolutionaries who will demand rapid change instead of tired rhetoric.

Even as kids, Cappy Plutos will know how to manage finances, understanding that she who controls the bank account controls the planet. By the time they're teens, they'll be lending money from their secret stash of cash hidden under the closet floor—for a reasonable interest rate—to their parents and friends. They will fight for the underdogs and work for equality, paving an easier path for future generations to follow.

Pluto in Aquarius (2023–2044)

We're on the brink of the Age of Aquarius, and Pluto's move into this humanitarian and rebellious sign will result in a further push for the common good.

Science and technology will advance at a breakneck pace as this generation strives to end world hunger, cure disease, and explore space. Sudden, radical changes may occur in governments and countries as these intellectual rebels push the ideals of the Capricorn-Plutos to total revolution against everything that oppresses the masses.

Don't be surprised if, under this group's guidance, the world reaches a new level of awareness so that the collective human brainpower can be focused on not only saving this planet, but contacting extraterrestrial life and striding outward, into the stars.

Pluto in Pisces (2042–2066)

The world may see a revival in magic, alchemy, and holistic spiritual beliefs from the Pluto-Pisces group that compliments the tech-crazy world of the Pluto-Aquarians. The world could also see an explosion of music and art during this period.

This generation will believe in universal love and perhaps clear the way for a resurgence of environmental well-being across the globe as well as a focus on our connection with the world around (and the worlds beyond) us.

Now that you've looked at Pluto through the wide-angle focus of his influence on your generation, it's time to increase the power on your imaginary telescope and start zeroing in on what this bad boy has in store for you personally, not just as a member of the masses.

PART TWO

The Sun Signs

Whether you're a casual daily-horoscope reader or a devoted astrology buff, chances are you know your sign. There are twelve zodiac signs, and each has its own characteristics, motivations, and behaviors. Are you a curious Gemini? A thoughtful Cancer? Perhaps a dedicated Capricorn? Your Sun sign represents your inner character. Although no two astrology charts are exactly alike, everything begins with the Sun, and everyone born under a certain sign will share some basic traits.

Depending on your Sun sign and what house Capricorn occupies in your natal chart, Pluto will flex his transformative muscles in your life in one or more of that house's themes. And—depending on how much work you need to do—your transit can start with a jolt, a speed bump, or a heart-pounding crisis. That's how Pluto gets your attention, but it's not all bad. For example: For all Aries people, Pluto in Capricorn is moving through your Tenth House of Career and Public Life. The themes in this house concern the balance between your public and private lives. Social status is also a tenth-house issue. Under his hard-driving influence, you'll be less inclined to be the company doormat and more inclined to stand up for yourself. You could decide to change jobs or start a new career. You could also see real rewards for all those years of sweat equity.

At the end of each Sun sign section you will find a brief look at what to look forward to and what to watch out for as Pluto moves through Capricorn, as well as a roadmap pointing you toward the specific house chapter that provides deeper insights. Don't forget to also read the chapter for your rising sign too!

Some Basics About Your Sun Sign

The Sun signs are grouped into four Elements (Fire, Earth, Air, and Water), three Qualities/Modalities (Cardinal, Mutable, and Fixed), and two Polarities (Masculine and Feminine).

The Elements

Fire signs are action driven. Aries, Leo, and Sagittarius live in the moment. They are prone to sudden bursts of passionate enthusiasm and aren't afraid to take risks. These characters like a varied routine, both in their work and personal lives. They are usually spontaneous and fun loving, but they can also be arrogant and self-centered. Though their tempers are prone to flare up, their anger fades quickly, and they rarely hold long-term grudges.

Earth signs are cautious. Taurus, Virgo, and Capricorn are slow to embrace change. Instead of jumping at new prospects, they require time to investigate their options before making a decision. Their natures are entwined with the sensual pleasures of food, textures, visual beauty, and scent. Although they lean toward caution and practicality in life, these individuals never take their eyes off the bottom line. Accumulating possessions makes them feel safe.

Air signs are analytical. Gemini, Libra, and Aquarius have to discuss all the angles—sometimes more than once—before making a move. This bunch is social and friendly. They love to talk about themselves and give advice to others. Often, they think they have all the answers but get in trouble when they embellish or ignore the facts. Frequently, they rationalize their own bad behaviors while criticizing the same conduct in their friends. Air signs like variety and often have several interests, jobs, or lovers to keep them busy.

Water signs are sensitive. Cancer, Scorpio, and Pisces see the world filtered through their emotions. They are intuitive and often absorb the feelings of family, friends, or crowds. This group needs frequent periods of solitude to help balance their lives. The Water signs are fiercely loyal to the people they love, sometimes to their own detriment, because of their tendency to live in denial of the truth.

The Qualities/Modalities

Cardinal signs initiate. Aries, Cancer, Libra, and Capricorn are spontaneous and forceful. These people are usually self-motivated and ambitious. They can also be domineering and temperamental.

Fixed signs stabilize. Taurus, Leo, Scorpio, and Aquarius are reliable. They have strong opinions and can be stubborn, but they are also patient and loyal.

Mutable signs adapt. Gemini, Virgo, Sagittarius, and Pisces are flexible. They can see both sides of a situation and thrive on change. This group is resourceful but restless.

The Polarities

Masculine (outgoing) signs act. Aries, Gemini, Leo, Libra, Sagittarius, and Aquarius are straightforward communicators, sometimes hot-tempered and/or domineering.

Feminine (receptive) signs react. Taurus, Cancer, Virgo, Scorpio, Capricorn, and Pisces are passive communicators, and can be manipulative and vague.

The following table gives you a quick guide to the basic nature of each Sun sign.

SIGN	ELEMENT	QUALITY	POLARITY
Aries	Fire	Cardinal	Masculine
Taurus	Earth	Fixed	Feminine
Gemini	Air	Mutable	Masculine
Cancer	Water	Cardinal	Feminine
Leo	Fire	Fixed	Masculine
Virgo	Earth	Mutable	Feminine
Libra	Air	Cardinal	Masculine
Scorpio	Water	Fixed	Feminine
Sagittarius	Fire	Mutable	Masculine
Capricorn	Earth	Cardinal	Feminine
Aquarius	Air	Fixed	Masculine
Pisces	Water	Mutable	Feminine

You'll feel Pluto's snarky hand twisting around your Sun and rising signs through the house he occupies while in Capricorn (his current position), and the effect will impact you in a more personal way than that of his trip through your generation. Understanding how his power can affect you through your Sun or rising sign can help you to prepare for a possible Pluto quake. Now that you have the basics, let's take a sign-by-sign look at the best and worst of the zodiac, and at Pluto's potential impact.

Aries (March 21–April 19)

Symbol: The Ram
Element: Fire
Quality: Cardinal
Polarity: Masculine
Ruler: Mars (Ares)
The Good: Enthusiastic, straightforward
The Bad: Bratty, quick-tempered
The Ugly: Aggressive, insensitive

ARIES

A Snapshot of Your Sign

Robin Hood was probably an Aries. He didn't like authority figures, preferred to live in the forest as an outlaw than to be just another voiceless subject, and he loved rescuing people—especially beautiful damsels.

Thanks to Mars, the warrior planet, you have that same independent spirit. Mixing it with action-oriented Fire and the self-reliant Cardinal Quality gives you a courageous, competitive soul that's always looking ahead to the next conquest or contest. However, living in the First House of Self turns much of this fiery energy inward, so that you wind up in pissing contests with yourself as much as with others.

The Aries symbol of the headstrong Ram manifests through your strong will. Whether quiet or annoyingly bossy, all Rams seldom give up until they get their way.

Willful You

Think of your favorite movie villain. He's totally committed to his life of crime and motivated to win at any cost. You may not be a villain, but boy, are you always motivated to win. In fact, you're as straightforward as a freight train. Whether you're on a quest to find your true love or cruising the bars for a one-night stand, once you set your sights on someone, you never give up.

The trouble is that you're so competitive that you never let your crush make the first move—or have the last word. That's why you either end up with a wuss (whom you walk all over) or you end up alone, because anyone with a backbone hits the pavement once you flip into boss mode. But that's okay with you, because you're also an adrenaline junkie who loves living on the edge.

Yours is a Masculine sign, and Mars, the warrior god that rules Aries, infused you with an overactive ego and giant-size need to run the show. Whether trying to rearrange a group tour to suit your schedule or just lording over your coworkers when the boss is away, you were born with a need to tell the rest of the world what to do. Maybe you're the quiet type who wouldn't think of disrupting the group or pushing your way to the front of a line. How nice. You might not raise your voice. You might not even argue—much. But the truth is that you'll get your way as often as any tantrum-tossing Aries. You're just smarter about how you handle the situation. You finagle. You charm. You do anything you must because, just like your hotheaded leader, you refuse to lose.

Whether you're pushing your body to the limit in a triathlon or badgering your boss for a raise, you can't stand second place. However, your responsibility skills aren't the sharpest tools in your arsenal. You're often as fickle as a Gemini. The difference is that a Gemini can't resist sampling everything. You always think the next job or the next hottie who catches your eye is going to be your perfect match, but as soon as you've made your conquest, you lose interest, which is why you often find yourself up to your eyeballs in angry ex-lovers. One may want your head on a pike while another tries to drag you to couples therapy. Neither will succeed. You're the universe's best escape artist. Surprisingly, once the tears dry and the dust settles, you're one of the signs who can remain friends with old partners and former spouses—that is, if you remember their names.

Warrior You

You're the most enthusiastic sign in the universe. Your symbol is the Ram, which means boundless energy. Aries is a Cardinal sign, which means leadership. And you're a Fire sign, which equals action. Mix these traits together and the ideal result is a self-confident, self-motivated, independent whiz kid. Muddle the brew, however, and you get a self-centered bully who demands constant attention. You probably fit somewhere between these extremes.

Mars was the Roman god of war and protection. He's both the aggressor and the hero, and you inherited both traits. Life can be either an adventure or a battlefield, but it's rarely dull. Although you're ready to fight at the drop of a careless word, you aren't violent. You just have zero tolerance for anyone or anything that stands in your way. You'll also never hesitate to fight for the underdog.

Aries's home on the zodiac wheel is the First House of Self. Your soul's greatest fear is that of being abandoned. In this life, you're learning how to develop your own identity and not take every disagreement or disappointment as personal rejection. The warrior side of you loves to compete, and your childlike soul needs to win because it associates winning with acceptance. When you win, you get your head patted. No other sign—not even ego-driven Leo—craves praise more than you. To you, praise equals love, which is why you have a soul-deep need to be the most popular kid on the block.

The first house represents the beginning of the soul's journey around the zodiac wheel. Like a baby who thrives on its parents' approval, you need reassurance from people you respect and recognition from those in authority. Astrology paints you as a go-getter who's always elbowing your way to the front of the line—and that's partially true. You can be driven to succeed on the job but let your partner make most of the decisions at home. Then, instead of the wolf in sheep's clothing, you're a gentle lamb disguised as a Ram.

Charisma is your best weapon, and you use it as relentlessly as a used-car salesman closing a deal. You'd never admit to using it, however, because you'd rather be labeled a bitch or a jerk than show any vulnerability. That gut reflex to spit on someone who wounds you is your self-defense mechanism. Of course that doesn't stop you from having a screaming fit or putting a fist through the nearest wall. But your anger is anxiety driven.

On the job, if you don't get the promotion or the sale or the new client, or if you lose the argument at home, you go into fight-or-flight mode. "Screw you, I'm leaving!" and "Screw you, I quit!" are your go-to howls when you feel cornered. This all-or-nothing attitude might make you look tough to others, but inside, you're just a little kid operating from hurt feelings and fear.

Real rams bash their horns to show their strength. You emotionally bash your metaphorical ones against anything that threatens your somewhat fragile ego. Aries rules the head, and it's your most vulnerable body part. Stress-induced tension headaches or migraines can be a real issue for you, so you must learn how to think first then react. One way to balance your hotheaded impulsiveness is by learning about your opposite sign, Libra.

You're the sign of self, and Libra, your opposite, lives in the Seventh House of Partnerships: Aries *I* versus Libra *We*. You need relationships but can have trouble telling the difference between love and lust. Once the passion cools and you unlock the handcuffs, the romance can fizzle as fast as it flared. On the flip side, you may fall into the role of protector, which is fine at the beginning, as you love to play the hero. But you also love to be the boss. When you batter your loved ones with orders and contradict everything they say, your bad behavior earns you a well-deserved breakup. Sure, it may not be for long, there are plenty of masochists around. If you keep it up, however, you'll eventually end up alone.

Lessons to learn from Libra are how to listen and negotiate. Libra's give-and-take traits create balance. When you can combine Libra's art of finesse with your heroic spirit, you'll be a true spiritual warrior.

Pluto and You

Until 2024, Pluto in Capricorn is moving through every Aries' Tenth House of Career and Public Life. Capricorn is the sign of tradition and power, and as you know, Pluto is the planet of behind-the-scenes control and upheaval. When these two meet in the tenth house, playing by the rules becomes critical. Pluto's transit can boost your drive and ambition. The catch is that he'll also test your ability to play fair as well as expose any contradictions between your public and private lives. Be sure to read about the tenth house in part three for a deeper look at some of the challenges and opportunities for all Aries and Aries-rising birthdays.

Taurus (April 20–May 20)

Symbol: The Bull
Element: Earth
Quality: Fixed
Polarity: Feminine
Ruler: Venus (Aphrodite)
The Good: Generous, loyal
The Bad: Stubborn, greedy
The Ugly: Judgmental, unforgiving

TAURUS

A Snapshot of Your Sign

When Venus visited Earth, she fell in love with every material and sensual pleasure. The moment you were born, so did you. You adore comfort and want your physical surroundings to be cozy.

The symbol of the peaceful Bull represents both your appreciation of humankind's earthy nature and its territorial trait. You're at home in the Second House of Money and Values. What you love, you own (at least, that's the way you'd like things to be). Money's only a means to an end for you. The possessions you buy with it make you feel secure.

Your Fixed Earth nature is loyal and kind. You hate change and often have to be pushed out of your comfort zone before you'll attempt anything new. Once you do, you own the idea as if it had been yours all along.

Bullish You

You're an enigma. Although you inherited Venus's love of comfort, her lazy streak, and her appreciation for expensive toys, you were off chasing a foot-long hoagie when she handed out her sense of style. The flair for fashion went to Libra, the other Venus-ruled Sun sign. Instead of a choosing from a rack of coordinated clothes hanging neatly in the closet, you dig your daily outfit out of the moldering pile of rags tossed in the corner of your bedroom. Does most of your dinner end up on your clothes instead of in your mouth? That's no surprise, as Bulls tend to overindulge in everything, including food and drink.

You love a cozy home, but keeping it clean is as unnatural to you as turning down a free meal. When it comes to housework, you have a dual dilemma. You hate to pay for a professional to scrub the toilets because you don't want to spend the money. More than that, you think one of your friends or family members should do it for you. No matter how sweet you seem on the surface, a big part of you believes that the world was created for your pleasure, and the people in it were born to serve you.

You really don't care if the sheets haven't been washed in a month or that pile of junk mail on your kitchen table creates a fire hazard. Baby, you're nature's child. To you, going without a bath for a week and wearing the same jeans until both knees (and even a bit of butt cheek) show through the tatters is perfectly normal.

Taurus is the sign of money and values. You value other people's money. It's not that you're tight fisted—you'll give someone you love your last dollar. However, you have Venus's talent for sniffing out people you can tap like an ATM when you need some cash. This isn't necessarily a bad trait, because you usually pay back the loan. But you can get into the habit of relying on other people to continually bail you out of one crisis after another. If expecting your friends and family to come to your rescue isn't enough, you have the nasty habit of turning into a raging bull when anyone dares to tell you enough already.

Your Venus-ruled psyche expects to be treated as if you were ruler of the universe. In reality, you should be handled like somebody who's one step away from a meltdown. Forget touchy Scorpio. The coffeehouse barista swirls the cream in your latte counterclockwise? Well, there goes your morning—ruined. A friend reminds you that your last three online affairs with convicted felons ended badly? She gets the silent treatment for a week. Everything offends you.

Although you'd never admit it, that's why you and Cancer make such a good team. As the zodiac's perpetual victims, there's nothing more fun for you than complaining about how hard you try to please the world without getting even a thank you in return.

But you are generous, and will go out of your way to help a pal without a thought of being repaid. Almost. On the surface, you tell yourself that it's okay that you've picked up the last six lunch tabs for your broke friend, but inside, your mind is clicking off the ratio of your money to their reciprocation. Does your chum even offer to pay you back? Buy dessert? Bring you a cheap gift? You're slow to anger, but once you feel that you're being taken for that proverbial ride, you slam the goodwill door in your pal's face. And you keep the doggy bag.

Soulful You

Your symbol is the macho Bull, but you're a Feminine sign. Of course, when you want something, you can be as intimidating as a real bull. However, your soul operates by the law of attraction. You're seductive—that's Venus's influence. You're also a little sneaky—Jupiter's (Zeus's) gift.

When Jupiter saw Europa, the princess of Phoenicia, he fell into instant lust. When he made a pass at her, she blew him off. She didn't care that he was head god of Mount Olympus, she knew his playboy reputation and wanted no part of that action. So, Jupiter disguised himself as a beautiful-but-wild white bull and seduced her by letting her think she'd tamed him. She scratched his ears. He rolled his huge brown eyes and nuzzled her hand. She wove a wreath of flowers around his neck. He kneeled so she could climb on his back and take a ride through the meadows. *Took her for a ride* is the key phrase. Jupiter charged straight for Crete, where he turned back into himself and made her his lover. You have the same appeal—the same talent for appearing to be docile when you're really a force of nature.

Although you can bellow like a real bull when angry, it takes a lot of prodding to make you lose your temper. In fact, you'll often make yourself sick rather than have a nasty confrontation. Taurus rules the throat, vocal chords, neck areas, and ears. When stressed, you can get a sore throat or ear infection. You might have allergies that make you hoarse or suffer from sneezing fits. Often, these conditions appear when you're upset but don't want to cause a fight. You choke on the words you're reluctant to say. Patience is a virtue, but try not to hold in your frustration until you get sick or explode in anger.

As Fixed Earth, your basic character is tenacious. You cling like moss to the people, ideas, and lifestyle that make you feel secure. Although you have plenty of casual chums, your best friends are people you've known most of your life. Think of a deeply-rooted oak tree. As long as it's not transplanted, it thrives. Change, even when it's positive, makes you nervous. However, once the facts have been hammered home, or you're forced to make a move, you instantly flip into *I own this* mode. The idea becomes yours, and no one can make you think differently.

Venus, the goddess of love and money, rules Taurus. Her energy is harmonious, and so is yours. Your inner nature is peaceful and patient, and Venus has infused you with her sensual nature. Yes, you're a sexy sign, known for both your loving heart and your between-the-sheets stamina, but Venus also loves comfort and luxury. So do you. Whether your bank account is bursting or you clip coupons to make ends meet, you ensure that your home is comfortable and welcoming. Scents, tastes, and textures all make you feel calm. Most Taureans love food and, with little effort, can become wonderful cooks.

Taurus lives in the Second House of Money and Values. Material possessions make you feel secure, and many Taureans are dedicated collectors. In the second house, the soul is like a toy-obsessed toddler. *Mine* is your operative word. Some Bulls have trouble getting rid of anything, including clothes from high school and gifts they hate. You can even have the I-don't-want-you-but-no-one-else-can-have-you attitude toward ex-lovers and former friends.

Your opposite sign, Scorpio, lives in the Eighth House of Shared Resources, Sex, and Inheritance. *Ours* is a key word of the eighth house. Where you connect security with tangible items, Scorpio associates security with emotional connections. You have a natural power over the physical world, but you can amass so much physical clutter that you stall. If you clear the messes from your overstuffed closet to long-dead relationships, you'll kick-start your soul's growth. Instead of self-indulgence, you'll learn the value of self-worth. When you balance your needs with the needs of others, you'll gain insight not only into their motivations but into yours.

Pluto and You

Until 2024, Pluto in Capricorn is moving through every Taurus's Ninth House of Philosophy, Travel, and Knowledge. Capricorn is the sign of tradition and power. Pluto is the planet of behind-the-scenes control and upheaval. In Capricorn, Pluto is trined to your Sun sign, which is a positive aspect because you and Capricorn are both Earth signs and have a natural affinity. You could have a chance to travel abroad or advance your education, and these years could bring you luck in all ninth-house areas—with one caution. Legal issues live in the ninth house, so be extra diligent about obeying the law. Read more about the ninth house in part three for a deeper look at some of the challenges and opportunities of Pluto's visit for all Taurus and Taurus-rising birthdays.

Gemini (May 21–June 20)

Symbol: The Twins
Element: Air
Quality: Mutable
Polarity: Masculine
Ruler: Mercury (Hermes)
The Good: Curious, friendly
The Bad: Gossipy, unreliable
The Ugly: Phony, caustic

A *Snapshot of Your Sign*

Five minutes after Mercury hit the air, he knew everything about everyone. You were born with the same insatiable curiosity, and living in the Third House of Communication gives you a gift for both listening and asking the right questions. Before you get through the checkout line at the grocery store, you know the life history of the guy standing next to you in line. You hear the latest employee gossip from the checker and discover that the unmarried and pregnant bag girl is slapping the boss with a paternity suit. By the time you get home, you could write a book. You're a people magnet—they love you and, for the most part, you love them (or at least you love to talk to and about them). Your Air Element gives you a sociable nature, and your Mutable Quality expresses itself through your symbol, the Twins. This means that you can see both sides of an argument or argue either side of an issue. However, your twin nature often causes you to have serious arguments with yourself. You're also capable of changing your mind, your plans, or your lovers without warning.

Flaky You

Whether you're changing jobs, clothes, or lovers, the only consistent thing about you is your inconsistency. By the time you're twenty, you've learned to live out of boxes because you move so often that you can't be bothered to unpack. Unpacking would cut into your party time!

You're ruled by Mercury, the messenger god, who controlled the flow of information. He was also a con artist and accomplished liar. So are you. That's fine because you consider being the fastest mouth in town a gift. Although your opposite sign, Sagittarius, can probably outtalk you in a blather contest, she rarely lies. To you, lying is just another part of speech. Even though you demand that others be straight with you and you can't stand a liar, you won't hesitate to stretch the truth until it snaps back in your face. This is because your fibs are as exaggerated as your idea of your own importance. Want a day off? Instead of just calling in sick, you invent a dying-relative story complete with gory details. Of course, anyone who's known you for more than five minutes has already heard some version of this tale.

Mercury circulated messages and news around the heavens but often omitted the facts in favor of cherry-picking the juiciest details. Besides, the truth is usually so boring. That's why you have the reputation of a walking gossip rag. You spread the latest rumors around town, and you have no trouble broadcasting the details of your personal life as well. No matter how much you swear to keep quiet, you just can't keep your mouth shut. You're described as not having very many long-term friends because you are too fickle to form lasting relationships. What really happens is that your pals back off because they get tired of having to monitor what they tell you for fear of becoming the next viral sensation on the internet.

As an Air sign, you're supposed to be logical, but you're actually one of the most irrational creatures under the Sun. And as a Mutable sign, you're more reactive than proactive. Although you have the capacity to see both sides of any argument, your overactive imagination makes you more than a little paranoid. If you run into your ex twice in the same day and he happens to nod in your direction both times, you think he's stalking you. Then your mind runs wild. Soon you're calling your friends, the police, and flagging down strangers to help save your life. While you're giving a statement to the cop and thanking the guy who stopped to rescue you, you decide they're both cuties you'd like to know better. So you take each one aside and invite him to dinner, and before long, you're in the middle of hot affairs with both of them. Of course, this leads to another disaster and the whole scenario starts again—but you don't mind. You're thinking of all the delicious stories you'll get to tell.

Charming You

You crackle with Mercury's exuberant energy. Yes, you may be a little too candid at times, but as a Masculine sign, you're rarely reluctant to say what's on your mind. Your cheerful smile and nonthreatening approach puts people at ease. So even if you're breaking up with your lover or telling a chum that he's being spiteful, you seldom have to resort to raising your voice.

Along with Mutable Water, Pisces, you're a dual sign. However, unlike Pisces's Fishes, which are often represented as swimming in opposite directions, the Gemini Twins face life side by side.

Castor and Pollux were the twin brothers of the mortal Leda, the wife of Tyndareus, the king of Sparta. Though Castor was born human like their mother (fathered by the king), Pollux was the product of roving-eyed Jupiter (Zeus), who seduced Leda by disguising himself as a swan. Pollux received his father's immortality. There are so many descriptions of this tale that you might say these two boys were the source of a wild gossip fest in the heavens. Despite the chin wagging, they were inseparable. When Castor was killed in battle, Pollux begged Jupiter to exchange his life for his brother's. True to the duality of this sign, one version of the story says that Jupiter allowed the twins to live on the Earth one day and then spend the next in Hades. The alternate version is that he rewarded their love for each other by placing them in the heavens as the constellation Gemini.

Instead of splitting yourself into the *should I or shouldn't I* con-fusion of Pisces, your twin-soul nature doesn't contradict itself. Instead, your third-house soul can be compared to an overconfident teenager, who's curious and eager to explore their immediate world but still needs an anchor of safety. Your Mutable Air is social like airy Libra. However, Libra's aim is to build relationships. You thrive on new experiences. Think of a steady breeze that circulates around every leaf and building. Whether at work or in your personal life, there's nothing you hate more than routine. Exchanging ideas and information keeps you in the know about what's going on in your world, but your curiosity can get out of hand.

The major body area Gemini rules is the nervous system, and you frequently overload yours with too much outside stimuli. You may be prone to chronic anxiety or full-blown panic attacks, which make you feel as if you're suffocating. Other areas are the lungs, hands, and arms. Too much texting or keyboarding can cause carpal tunnel symptoms. Slowing down a bit is the secret to maintaining your wellbeing. Take a hint from the other Mercury-ruled sign, Virgo, and try to become more organized while paying attention to your mental health.

Gemini has the reputation for being scattered. Your soul wants to learn, process, and pass on knowledge as fast as possible, which can overload your human brain. You're known as a multitasking wizard, and that's mostly true. Although you can juggle romance, projects, and family responsibilities better than most people, you often skim the surface without taking the time to be thorough. Mer-cury communicated at the speed of sound, but the price of speed is a lack of depth.

Sagittarius, your opposite sign, lives in the Ninth House of Phi-losophy, Travel, and Knowledge. This Mutable-Fire Archer is also social and outgoing. Both of you are logical and seek knowledge. The difference between you is that Sagittarius's Fire is more focused and detailed than Gemini's Air energy. You can be easily distracted by trivia, and Sagittarius likes to solve one problem before moving to the next. Your mental processes are grounded in everyday life, whereas Sagittarius looks for deeper connection and meaning. Your challenge is to learn how to balance your talent for hatching brilliant ideas with self-discipline and follow through.

Pluto and You

Until 2024, Pluto in Capricorn is moving through every Gemini's Eighth House of Shared Resources, Sex, and Inheritance. Capricorn is the sign of tradition and power. Pluto is the planet of behind-the-scenes control and upheaval. As the eighth house is Pluto's natural home on the zodiac wheel, during this transit, you're completely on his turf. And this journey can be rough because you will come face to face with people and situations that reflect some of your worst traits. Joint finances, money you owe, and emotional and tangible legacies are part of the eighth house. Read about the eighth house in part three for a deeper look at some of the challenges and opportunities of Pluto's visit for all Gemini and Gemini-rising birthdays.

Cancer (June 21–July 22)

Symbol: The Crab
Element: Water
Quality: Cardinal
Polarity: Feminine
Ruler: The Moon
The Good: Caring, protective
The Bad: Moody, irritable
The Ugly: Manipulative, suffocating

CANCER

A Snapshot of Your Sign

Moonlight represents romance and tender emotions, and you're full of both. Water represents empathy and deep feelings. These traits are also part of your nature. The Cardinal Quality is responsible, which makes Cancers feel the need to care for others. Finally, the Fourth

House of Home and Family is home to your sign. Is it any wonder you have a soul-deep desire to protect and defend the ones you love as well as offer help and comfort to perfect strangers? The Crab, your zodiac symbol, is a shy creature that carries its home on its back. Wherever you go in life, you carry in your heart memories of home and those you've loved.

Moody You

When the Moon and the Sun merged into your sign, the resulting explosion of emotional excess gave you a perpetual penchant for high drama. Never mind Scorpio's brooding or theatrical Leo's demand for attention, your drama magnet's strong enough to shift the Earth's magnetic field. Although you cry to everyone within earshot about your horrible life, you secretly like the angst because pity parties are your favorite pastime.

Throughout history and across cultures, the Sun and the Moon have been said to be lovers. Some tales say that the elusive Moon led the passionate Sun on a merry chase around the Earth. The closest he ever got was to catch a glimpse of her vanishing beneath the far horizon just as he was lighting the sky each morning. Her subtle charm and muted glow kept him running in circles forever. Sweet, but you're about as subtle as a whiney three-year-old. As for muted, do you think those muffled sobs and stricken looks count? They might—if they weren't so carefully calculated.

You're as touchy-feely as Scorpio and Pisces, the other two Water signs. However, you're Cardinal Water, which means you're not only sensitive, you're bossy. And manipulative. *And* sneaky.

You're as greedy as your opposite sign, Capricorn, only you prefer to push your partner to the limit, eventually requiring him or her to work overtime so you can play the happy homemaker. You will go to any lengths to avoid working for a living. Migraines. Panic attacks. Vague illnesses that only hit during the busy season. And after a few years, you can't hold a job longer than six months without having a nervous breakdown. Finally, your honey gives in, and you get to stay home—only that's no fun either, because when you're alone all day, your imagination runs rampant. Perhaps you picture your partner screwing a coworker in the supply closet. Soon, you're thinking up lame excuses to call every hour, which then causes trouble with the boss and battles to begin at home. Soon, your babe really is having an affair, and you're headed for the nearest therapist. But, of course, this thrills you to no end—playing the tragic hero of your own life is a million times more fun for you than seeing your name in lights on a Broadway marquee.

Despite your reputation as a nurturer, your family life resembles a survival boot camp, with you as head drill sergeant. Although this sounds contradictory to you being the victim, it isn't. When your loved ones walk in the door, none of them knows whether they're going to be greeted with a kiss or a cleaver. Your lovers, friends, and relatives learn to duck first and check your mood later. And their attempts at self-preservation keep you in a constant state of turmoil. You keep smooching and swinging the blade in equal turns as they keep cringing and ducking. Soon, everyone's on the verge of a genuine nervous breakdown—except you. Secretly, the more chaotic life is, the better you like it. The reason behind the messes you always attract can be found in the story of the most dysfunctional family in the universe.

Cancer, the Crab, was loyal to Juno (or Hera in Greek mythology), Queen of the Olympians, who was Jupiter's (Zeus's) wife. Jupiter was the first philandering husband, and he went after everything he could charm or trick into bed. Although Juno was used to his cheating, she was incensed when she learned of his affair with a mortal woman—Alcmene—and that the situation resulted in the birth of the hero Hercules (Heracles). Juno hated Hercules. From the time he was born, she tried to kill him. Finally, she sent the giant crab, Cancer, to distract him while he was on his quest to destroy the multiheaded Hydra. When Cancer scuttled out of its hiding place to nip Hercules's heels, Hercules managed to smash its shell and destroy it. As a reward for its loyalty, Juno turned the giant crab into one of the zodiac's constellations.

As a Cancer, you are loyal, but when it comes to someone you care about, you can be totally irrational. If you've misplaced your trust, you're as crushed as the giant Crab—only you seldom learn the lesson. Of all the signs, you'll stay in bad relationships the longest. The trouble is that you say you forgive, but you never forget. You suffer regular flashbacks about your cheating spouse or the friend who betrayed you. Then you and everyone around you have to relive the pain. Although you'll fight to the end for your loved ones, you expect the same blind loyalty in return. And you'll pull every heartstring within reach until you get it.

Devoted You

Yes, your moods are as changeable as the phases of your ruler the Moon, but your compassion is as limitless as the stars. As a Water sign, you feel first then think, which intensifies your sensitive nature. Cancer is a Feminine sign and lives in the Fourth House of Home and Family. The Moon symbolizes motherhood and represents the core of your emotional nature. Can you see why you were born with a need to nurture and protect, and sometimes meddle in the lives of the ones you love?

In the fourth house, the soul seeks security through family ties. This house also represents your physical home. However, the concept that Cancers are stuck in tradition and would rather stay by the fireplace than socialize is completely wrong. Just as many Cancers love travel and adventure as any of the other signs. You also have a quirky and hilarious sense of humor and can get as down and dirty as anyone. Think of Robin Williams or Will Ferrell. The idea that all Cancers sit around at home, sobbing at TV commercials and trying to chain their kids to their ankles, is ridiculous.

You were born with an instinct to shelter the people you care about because everyone you care about is included in your extended family. And you have a large one. Coworkers, friends, the checkout person at the grocery store, your boss, the kids next door—the list goes on and on. Contrary to the negative portrait of you as bossy and manipulating, you're one of the most softhearted signs in the zodiac. That's how you get into trouble.

As a Cardinal sign, you believe you know best, but when a crisis occurs, you get so involved that you often can't think logically. Take a lesson from your opposite sign, Capricorn: the Goat lives in the Tenth House of Career and Public Life—a totally public place. The fourth house is private. Capricorn is Cardinal Earth and is also inclined to tell others what to do. However, Capricorn is less interested in others' feelings than in getting results.

You are a walking contradiction. As a Cardinal sign, you're action driven and naturally want to take the lead. As the Moon-ruled Water sign, you can't stand conflict. You strive for harmony because quarrels of any kind can make you physically ill. Cancer rules the breasts, stomach, and upper digestive tract. Under stress, you can either lose your appetite or go on a binge of constant nibbling. Either way, you upset your system. Turning your tension inward starts a vicious cycle of feeling sick and being super touchy. Save yourself a bellyache and your family a browbeating by learning to speak up instead of letting your imagination fester until you blow a minor issue way out of proportion.

Despite your deeply sensitive nature, you are strong and resilient. The key to unlocking your inner power is by learning to temper your extreme emotions with self-discipline. When you can harness your powerful sentiment so you don't self-destruct every time a challenge arises, you'll have the best of both worlds.

Pluto and You

Until 2024, Pluto in Capricorn is moving through every Cancer's Seventh House of Partnerships. Capricorn is your opposite sign and represents tradition and power. Pluto is the planet of secrets and upheaval. When Pluto moves through the seventh house, your closest personal relationships get shaken up. Although some unpleasant issues might be exposed, these years bring a wonderful opportunity to toughen up your heart in a good way and the chance to completely overhaul your deepest connections, making them stronger than ever. Read the section on partnership and the seventh house in part three for a deeper look at some of the challenges and opportunities of Pluto's visit for all Cancer and Cancer-rising birthdays.

Leo (July 23–August 22)

Symbol: The Lion
Element: Fire
Quality: Fixed
Polarity: Masculine
Ruler: The Sun
The Good: Protective, courageous
The Bad: Egotistical, bossy
The Ugly: Dictating, shallow

LEO

A Snapshot of Your Sign

The Sun gives life to our universe. The Lion is the king of the zodiac. This fiery combination gives you a generally sunny disposition and the need to be ruler of your world. You also love attention because your home on the zodiac wheel is the outgoing Fifth House of Creativity, Children, and Romance.

Just like a lion in the wild, you have a soul-deep need to be in control of your fate and the fate of your human pride. You love to control everyone in your world, from loved ones to coworkers, because you really think you know best. And to you, the easiest way to accomplish this is to keep your people close and direct their every move. This isn't because you're egotistical or selfish, however. As one of the Fixed signs, your loyalty runs deep. So, even if you're a quiet Leo who rarely loses your temper, you were born with fierce courage and won't hesitate to walk through fire to defend the ones you love.

Jungle-Cat You

Most astrologers call you the ruler of the jungle—the zodiac—just like the noble Lion, your zodiac symbol. Have you ever watched a wildlife documentary? Lions spend their days sleeping, their nights preying on the weak, and their spare time in perpetual heat. They also love to yowl just to hear themselves make noise.

As the human version of this lazy, belligerent bully, you demand affection from everyone you meet and sex from anyone who'll hold still long enough. The Sun rules Leo, and you act as if you have the same high-wattage brilliance. You think you're a sexy beast, but you can come off as an irritating pest.

Leo is the sign of creativity and ambition. However, your creative streak can be limited to inventing new ways to suck money out of your friends to finance your latest pyramid scheme.

You can be the zodiac's biggest spender. You love to pick up the check because it makes you feel important, and you're all about image. Even if you're a quiet Lion, you like to be boss—or at least think you are.

Your ruler, the Sun, is the most brilliant star in our solar system, and you need to shine in your life too. Leo lives in the Fifth House of Creativity, Children, and Romance. This is the home of fun, imagination, and recreational sex. And whether you're a bartender or a brain surgeon, you like to be the star of the show.

As with every wild thing, you occasionally like a roaring good fight. Of course, this clears the air. But try not to forget that other people's feelings and wishes are as important as your own.

You're as stubborn in your beliefs as your opposite sign, Aquarius, another of the Fixed signs. Only a major event can get you to change your opinion. Aquarius is Fixed Air, so she talks to get her point across. You're Fixed Fire and may throw a fit to make your case. However, you'd rather charm your opponent into submission whenever possible.

Lucky for you that you are so damn charming you can get away with outrageous behaviors that would get lesser Sun signs killed.

Noble You

Whether you're a quiet Lion who prefers evenings at home or as exuberant as a movie star hogging the camera, you crave attention. Just as the Sun is the center of our universe, you need to be the center of yours.

Your personality is usually as warm and welcoming as a sunny day. You're generous with your friends and faithful to your partners. You believe in happily ever after, but that's a duel-edged virtue because you can stay in a relationship that's long past its pull date. And it isn't because you're resigned to play the victim, as a Water sign will do. You just have a fairy-tale outlook on life. When your spouse turns to louse, or you find your squeeze's boots shoved under your roommate's bed, you're crushed.

Supposedly, when your pride's wounded, you walk out without a backward glance. Not true. You'll roar, you'll threaten. And not just to make a scene but to try to save the relationship. You aren't afraid to confront any situation, but your first goal is to repair the damage. Once you're certain you can't, then you'll leave—and you'll take everything from the cat to the bank account with you. No matter what happens, you always bounce back stronger. You have almost as much endless optimism as your fellow Fire sign Sagittarius.

More than that, your symbol is the courageous and fearsome Nemean Lion of Roman and Greek mythology, with skin so tough no weapon could pierce it. Killing the huge beast was one of Hercules's (or Heracles's) famous twelve labors, which were ordered by his cousin Eurystheus, the king of Tiryns. After a lengthy fight, Hercules succeeded in strangling it, but he lost a finger in the process. The Lion wasn't about to go down without a fight. To prove his success, Hercules was required to take the Lion's pelt back to Eurystheus. But since no weapon could cut its skin, Hercules's task was far from over. He finally figured out that only the beast's claws could penetrate its hide. And although the Lion lost its life, Juno (Hera), Jupiter's (Zeus's) wife, set it among the stars in the constellation Leo.

You're known for loving luxury and high living. But unlike some other signs that will drive themselves to bankruptcy court to have the latest gadgets and the biggest house on the block, you'll work yourself to death to create your ideal lifestyle. Leo rules the heart and back. Overwork, stress, and the frustration you can feel at not succeeding as quick as you think you should, can cause you to implode. Every Leo has an inner lazy lion. You must let your big cat out to nap, lie in the sun, and get pampered and petted in order to maintain your health.

You're Fixed Fire, and your emotions burn hot and steady. You're faithful to your lovers and friends, and won't hesitate to help someone in need in any way possible. Although you rarely expect payback for your kindnesses, you do require thanks. *Lots* of thanks. *Hero-worshipping* thanks. Your fifth-house soul seeks adoration, and unchecked egotism can be a big problem for you. When you get too full of your own hubris, your good deeds come across as superficial acts. Then your faithful followers turn into a mob of angry torchbearers.

Your opposite sign, Fixed-Air Aquarius, lives in the Eleventh House of Friends, Groups, and Wishes. While you may be concerned with what you can get from others, Aquarius is interested in doing what's best for the group. Your balance lies in merging your generous nature with the unpretentious goals of Aquarius. When that happens, you really will be the baddest beast on the block.

Pluto and You

Until 2024, Pluto in Capricorn is moving through every Leo's Sixth House of Everyday Work, Service, and Health. Capricorn represents the status quo and power; Pluto is the planet of upheaval. In the sixth house, Pluto stirs up on-the-job turmoil and reminds you to pay attention to your health. You could receive a significant reward or opportunity in your career. You might overcome a health issue or start living a very health-conscious lifestyle. Read about the "Phoenix of Service" in part three for a deeper look at some of the challenges and opportunities of Pluto's visit for all Leo and Leo-rising birthdays.

Virgo (August 23–September 22)

Symbol: The Virgin
Element: Earth
Quality: Mutable
Polarity: Feminine
Ruler: Mercury (Hermes)
The Good: Helpful, analytical
The Bad: Irritable, hypochondriacal
The Ugly: Hypercritical, negative

VIRGO

A Snapshot of Your Sign

When Mercury stepped onto the Earth, he lost some of his impatient, flaky nature and gained a sense of dedication to duty. As an Earth sign ruled by the king of the Air, you inherited the best of both worlds, and because you're a Mutable sign, you're social and like people, but your practical nature helps to keep you from overextending yourself.

Living in the Sixth House of Everyday Work, Service, and Health, you were born to help others and maintain an orderly routine. Your mind clicks with the precision of a Rolex. Whether tweaking grandma's brownie recipe or showing a friend how to pack for Hawaii, your intention is to make everything you touch better. The image of you as a perfectionist is a popular misconception. You're the zodiac's organizer. Routine and structure help to keep you calm. Without them, you bite your nails in nervous irritability. With them, you thrive. The moral to this story? Don't let anyone ever push you into hurrying a decision or rushing through a project.

Uptight You

There you sit, a pleated, pressed, and poised picture of perfection. An expectant smile plays across your face. Your hands are neatly folded in your lap. You've just finished privately advising three friends on the best way to get along with each other. Calm, friendly, caring—that's the Virgo image.

But if you remove the soft-focus lens, the real picture emerges. Your clothes are held together with safety pins. Your hands are clenched so no one sees the chewed, bloody stubs that used to be your fingernails. And the three friends you've just tried to help are tearing each other's hair out. What the hell happened?

You're a compulsive fixer. Whether you're counseling your pals, planning a cruise down the Amazon, or just trying to write a grocery list, you never know when to quit tweaking the process. By the time you're ready to pay a deposit, the ship's sailed. When you've finally decided on the two-for-one special on organic mung beans, both the sale and the beans have expired.

Your ruler, Mercury, is the charming communicator who brought the exchange of ideas to the universe. Mercury's natural habitat is Air. He flits around the zodiac delivering messages and chatting up the neighbors. Virgo's natural habitat is Earth, and when these two meet, it's like blowing a fan at a brick wall—lots of hot air and no forward motion.

Going out with your BFFs? You set a time. They arrive to pick you up. You ask them to wait a moment because you forgot to take your vitamins. Two hours later, after you've changed clothes, twisted your ankle stumbling over the cat, and searched the house for the coupons you thought were in your purse, you're ready. Meanwhile, your pals are in a coma on the couch from the fifth of gin they mainlined to keep from killing you.

You're described as a perfectionist, but you're more of a control freak. You're so busy trying to tweak everything—from the way the salt shaker sits in proximity to the pepper mill to driving endlessly around the mall looking for a parking space equal distance from each of your favorite stores—that you're blissfully unaware of anything else, including the mess your life can become when you don't pay attention.

Every sign can avoid the truth, but you're as oblivious as any Water sign when it comes to denying the facts. You've gained thirty pounds, and your relationship is in the toilet. What do you do? Stock up on pizza and buy a bigger bed so your paramour won't accidentally bump your butt during the night. Your partner is nuttier than a foil-hatted alien chaser. Do you suggest that visiting a shrink might help? No. Go to a therapist yourself? Uh-uh. Kick your honey out? Nope. You decide to nag the poor soul into sanity. As a Mutable sign, you're as longwinded as any Gemini and can ramble on longer than a Pisces on peyote. But by the time you've made your diagnosis, recited a list of psychoses, and created a treatment plan, your main squeeze really *has* contacted a UFO and fled to another planet.

Meticulous You

Let's get the facts straight. Virgo the Virgin is a laughable misnomer. The sweet-faced woman who symbolizes your sign more closely represents sensual Tellus (Gaia), Mother Earth than a pure-hearted innocent.

Virgo is the sixth sign of the zodiac and represents service and health. Although the sixth-house soul's focus is still on you as an individual, it's learning how to be useful to others—that's where you get your love for overhauling every person you meet. You may come across as critical, nitpicking, and obsessed with minutia, but your motivation is first and foremost to be helpful. You also need to stay busy. You're lost without a project to manage or a friend to help through a crisis.

Your earthly nature is grounded and wants security. Your airy ruler, Mercury, gives you a natural curiosity. When your Mercury intellect wants to explore and experiment, and your earthbound practicality tells you to use caution, you get into trouble. You're full of Mercury's restless energy, but your need to get the details can bog you down. When that happens, you get nervous and can make yourself ill.

Virgo rules your nervous system just as Gemini rules hers. However, your stress manifests in the lower digestive tract. You might suffer cramps or one of the maladies of the large intestine. Because you live in the Sixth House of Everyday Work, Service, and Health, it's crucial that you treat your body right with nutritious food and exercise, which you often don't do despite how you love to talk about your health. Although it's safe to say you're probably a walking pharmacy, your remedies seldom help when you're having one of your bouts of hypochondria. You may really feel and think you're sick when actually you're having an attack of contradictory impulses. Mercury's curious air wants to experiment, take risks, and forget the rules. That's good advice. Earthly Virgo warns you to be cautious and not make any mistakes, so you mentally beat yourself up and miss the fun.

No one's perfect. Make that your mantra and you'll feel a whole lot better.

You're at your best when you feel appreciated, and you'll do everything you can to make your friends and family happy. When you successfully combine your airy intellect and earthly common sense into a series of calculated risks, you can reap the benefits of both.

Pluto and You

Until 2024, Pluto in Capricorn is moving through every Virgo's Fifth House of Creativity, Children, and Romance. Capricorn represents tradition and power. Pluto is the planet of upheaval. In the fifth house, Pluto digs up issues with children or can bring a desire to have children. Pluto is trined to your Sun sign, which is a positive aspect because you and Capricorn are both Earth signs and have a natural affinity. A creative dream you put away years ago may resurface, bringing you lots of attention and opportunities. If so, with Pluto boosting your ego, you'll have the courage to take a chance. You could also experience a soul-shaking romance or renewed love in an existing relationship. Read the section in part three about Pluto in the fifth house for a deeper look at some of the challenges and opportunities of Pluto's visit for all Virgo and Virgo-rising birthdays.

Libra (September 23–October 22)

Symbol: The Scales of Justice
Element: Air
Quality: Cardinal
Polarity: Masculine
Ruler: Venus (Aphrodite)
The Good: Fair, thoughtful
The Bad: Self-absorbed, vain
The Ugly: Insensitive, narcissistic

LIBRA

A Snapshot of Your Sign

Venus rules both Libra and Taurus. In the Bull's case, she bestowed a love of the physical senses and a need for security gained through gathering money and possessions. In you, she instilled the love of beauty, the love of love itself, and a need to keep your world on an even keel. Your symbol, the Scales of Justice, represents your constant emotional balancing act. You're the zodiac's eternal romantic. Love is your primary word and at the root of everything you do. When forced to live in an unhappy situation, you wilt like a flower in the desert.

Your sign lives in the Seventh House of Partnerships. With Venus in control, you can't help but get deeply involved with everyone you meet. Work. Friendship. The life story of the parking-garage attendant. Every person in your life means something to you, and you do your best to help him or her in any way you can.

Manipulative You

You're on a hunt for the perfect lover, and you don't care how many relationships you destroy to find your fantasy. Although Venus gave you the power to charm almost any cutie out of some money and into your bed, the trouble is that you're as full of illusion as any Pisces.

Libra is the sign of balance and harmony—your symbol is the Scales of Justice—but you're forever trying to tip the scales in your favor. This is because you want to win as badly as your opposite sign, Aries. Both you and Aries are Cardinal signs, which means you like to have your way. The difference is that Aries Fire is always hot, always direct. Your Air Element snakes around corners and through cracks in the walls. Aries makes their intentions clear from the start. Libra makes friends with their target's partner first. You justify the innuendo-laden flirting as platonic good fun, of course—right up until the moment the jeans get unzipped. The reason you often fool yourself and others into thinking you're a pushover is because of that power of illusion.

You pride yourself on being fair-minded but have a talent for twisting every fact so that you never see the damage you do. The only time you face reality is when you're forced to—when your scales are so out of balance they crash to the ground. You say your best friend wants to rip your face off because you're sleeping with his girlfriend? Then and only then do you try to lay down a rational argument for your bad behavior. (In Libra-speak, *rational* translates to "lie your ass off to save it.")

Even if you don't get caught, the bounds of your love go only as far as how well you're treated by your lover. Should she dump you in favor of someone else or go back to your friend, you make her think you've bowed out gracefully. In reality, you wait a suitable length of time (in your mind)—ten or twenty minutes—before you invite your friend, whom you've betrayed, to lunch, where you turn on the drama as you clutch his hand and confess the affair. Photos optional.

You justify your treachery as the storybook romance you could not resist. "No one's at fault, it just happened." Yes, lots of people use that excuse, but you are the all-time champ. You'd rather be gnawed on by a zombie than assume blame for anything. Worse, after you've dropped this shattering news on your poor friend, you have the gall to tell him that you hope it doesn't ruin your friendship.

Meanwhile, you're still sneaking around, sending texts to your fling in hopes of winning her back—not because you want her but because you want to make her pay for dumping you. Of all the Sun signs, a Libra will try to keep an old lover dangling as long as possible just to prove that they can. You could hate her (and probably do, if you'd admit it), but you like to see just how much trouble you can cause. Her new relationship crumbles? Good. She comes crawling to you? Wonderful. You'll rationalize it all night, pretending to weigh the pros and cons of reconciling. Of course, you have no intention of taking anyone back. That's all part of your illusion.

You're described as a team player, but this is only true when you're leading the team. Venus is lazy. You inherited her distaste for work and prefer to surround yourself with drones who labor while you assume the position of queen bee. Whether you're a stay-at-home parent or the president of your own company, you measure your success by how many people are willing to put up with your incessant whining about life's unfairness and your latest hangnail. You're in a dead-end job. Your budget's out of control. Your partner's a pig. Your ass hurts from sitting around complaining all day. But do you *do* anything about it? Rarely. Although you're a Cardinal sign, which represents taking action, most of your action consists of flapping your jaw in hopes of getting sympathy.

Diplomatic You

The Scales of Justice that symbolize your Libra Sun sign represent your inner need for balance. To stay on an even keel, you work at being objective, trying to do what's best for everyone. You're described as vacillating—but that's not true. Your Cardinal Air just prefers to lead like the other Cardinal signs, and Venus gave you a special talent for negotiation. Libra's Masculine Polarity also means that, as nice as you are, you won't hesitate to speak out when you must. Add your sweet disposition, and the result is a tough-minded but usually reasonable diplomat.

Libra's mythology is connected to Justitia (or Astraea), the goddess of justice. Your symbol, the Scales of Justice, is the only astrological symbol not represented by a living creature. "Libra" is the name of the scales the goddess holds. Justitia is the daughter of Themis, the keeper of divine justice, and Jupiter (Zeus). The keeper of human justice, Justitia is said to have fled the Earth for the heavens when she grew tired of living among humanity's never-ending strife. She became the Virgo constellation so she could oversee from afar, and her scales became the Libra constellation. She is supposed to return one day to restore peace and balance to the world. This explains your need for balance in your life. Even when faced with sensitive issues, you always strive to weigh every angle and make the wisest decision possible.

However, as noble as your penchant for fairness seems, your ulterior aim is to avoid conflict. Only anxiety-ridden Pisces will run faster from a battle. Constantly trying to dodge unpleasant situations by refusing to take sides makes you seem phony, and then you just end up wondering what you did to make everyone so damned mad.

When these situations occur, look to your opposite sign—Aries. Certainly, Aries can be selfish and too quick to judge, but your attempt to be impartial usually results in you getting caught in the middle. Instead of studying every possible angle of the situation in hopes of achieving harmony, it's best to go with your instinct and take a stand. If you simply cannot do that, then bow out gracefully. Better to let your friends or family duke it out by themselves than try to referee and end up with two black eyes.

Libra governs the kidneys and lower back. The toxicity from stressful situations can build up in your system and result in bladder infections or kidney stones. Like Venus, you're prone to overindulging in rich food and drink, so it's crucial for you to maintain your health with a balanced diet and lifestyle.

The seventh sign of the zodiac, Libra dwells at the tipping point where the soul's focus shifts from being preoccupied with its individual desires to discovering how to get along with others. Part of your balancing act is learning how to tell the difference between generosity and selfishness. And this can become a real dilemma because your ruling force—Venus—was the smoothest operator in the universe.

Venus was the daughter of Uranus, or Father Sky, who had been attacked in a coup spearheaded by his son, Saturn (Cronus to the Greeks). By order of his mother, Tellus (or Gaia, Mother Earth), whose youngest children had been imprisoned by Uranus, Saturn castrated his father and threw his genitals deep in the ocean. It was from these that Venus was born. Although she immediately flew into the air and chose to live there, she's connected to the emotional power of the water. Venus was at her best when she was surrounded by beauty, culture, and delicious decadence—she invented the power of attraction. Taurus, the other Venus-ruled sign, is attracted to objects and people that make the Bull feel safe and secure. Taurus desires. In Libra, Venus attracts people that want to get close to you. Libra is desired. With so many people vying to be your pal, your lover, or your favorite relative, it's easy for you to become as vain as Venus. And this trap gets you into all sorts of trouble because you end up wanting to please everyone—especially yourself.

Whatever your interpersonal pitfalls may be, most of the time, you're the perfect partner. Even when you're being a brat, it's hard to dislike your warm-hearted good humor. As an Air sign, communication is important to you. As with Gemini and Aquarius, you like people. Gemini's curious about their lives, and Aquarius likes to observe them from a distance. Your Air-sign logic is tempered with sentiment, which enhances your talent for knowing the right thing to say in any situation. Your demeanor puts people at ease, and your romance-first outlook keeps your love life cozy. You are the zodiac's peacekeeper. When you're in top form, you not only keep the peace but nothing can keep you from getting anything—or anyone—you want.

Pluto and You

Until 2024, Pluto in Capricorn is moving through every Libra's Fourth House of Home and Family. Capricorn represents the status quo and power, and Pluto is the planet of transformation. When Pluto moves through the fourth house, both your idea of what home means and the physical place in which you live get revamped. This house also contains the memories of your childhood home. Part of Pluto's transformation of this house is to give you the courage to create your home just the way you want it without feeling guilty about breaking the bonds of family traditions. Read "Pluto in the Fourth House: The Phoenix of Nurturing" in part three for a deeper look at some of the challenges and opportunities of Pluto's visit for all Libra and Libra-rising birthdays.

Scorpio (October 23–November 21)

Symbol: The Scorpion
Element: Water
Quality: Fixed
Polarity: Feminine
Ruler: Pluto (Hades) and Mars (Ares)
The Good: Passionate, resourceful
The Bad: Suspicious, controlling
The Ugly: Vindictive, sullen

A Snapshot of Your Sign

Of all the zodiac signs, you're the most misunderstood. You're Fixed Water, ruled by mysterious Pluto, and you live in the shadowy eighth house. Your symbol, the Scorpion, is a scary little creature. All the dark and dangerous descriptions of your sign can make you feel like you were born with a sword hanging over your head. The truth is, you're one of the most sensitive souls in the universe, and like the Scorpion, you don't attack unless you're provoked.

You're described as secretive, but in reality, you are just a private person who doesn't vomit out your personal life to anyone who'll listen. What about sex-on-the-brain? Yes, you have the reputation for being a very sexual being, but what you truly desire is intimacy—body and soul together—in your relationships. On the surface, you may seem outgoing, but it takes you longer to develop deep feelings for someone. You even hold friendships at a distance until you're sure that you can trust the other person. And no one ever knows everything about you.

Suspicious You

You're the zodiac's emotional garbage dump. If you didn't have bad karma, you'd have no karma. However, as loudly as you sing the *Why me?* blues, you secretly crave the endless trauma. Like fellow Water sign, Cancer, you can't function in calm seas. Unless you're either running to your next lose-lose relationship or running from the last nutcase you met at Manipulators Anonymous, you're just not happy.

Mars, the god of war, and Pluto, the lord of the underworld, rule Scorpio. When the overeager energy of Mars is repressed by secretive Pluto, the result is a mix of anger and obsession. Just like Pluto, you are guarded and suspicious—more than a little paranoid. You were born knowing that *everyone* is out to get you. And you know what? You're right.

You come by that impulse naturally. Orion, the mortal who was handsome, charming, and the best hunter in the world, captured the attention of the goddess Diana (Artemis), also a great hunter. (Her silver-tipped arrows never missed their target.) Orion and Diana became friends, and during one of their hunts, Orion bragged that he could—and would—kill every wild beast on Earth. When Mother Earth—Tellus (Gaia)—heard this, she sent a giant scorpion to hunt the hunter. The battle between Orion and the scorpion was long and fierce, but the scorpion ultimately won, stinging the great hunter to death. To memorialize the hero, Diana requested that Jupiter, her father, make Orion a constellation. Jupiter agreed, but he also made a constellation of the scorpion as a reminder of Orion's defeat—a warning to all men that hubris will only turn them into mindless predators. To this day, the two live in opposite corners of the sky, unseen by the other but still in endless pursuit.

Although you were born with an instinct for tracking the truth of any situation, like your symbol, the Scorpion, you continually back yourself into corners that you have to fight your way out of because you're not an aggressive creature. When your Mars anger wants to lash out, your watery angst sucks you deeper into Pluto's emotional quicksand. Sooner or later, you spew a barrage of volcanic fury at the nearest human. You may hate your job, your family, or your dentist, but the sad fact is that you could have avoided all the drama if you weren't so guarded. You expect people to read your mind, and when they can't, you feel betrayed. Talking to you is like questioning a hostile witness. In fact, an easy way to recognize a Scorpio is to ask a direct question. The result is the same as throwing water on the Wicked Witch of the West. You melt away in a burst of steam.

Scorpio rules the reproductive organs, which is convenient for you because sexual crises are your favorite kind. You may put a lot of stock in your skill at wielding a little black whip, but you're no better at flirting or sex than any other sign. It's your well-practiced inscrutable smirk that makes your friends think you're getting it on with everyone from the UPS guy to your gynecologist. You want people to believe you had a weekend orgy when in reality you were flopped on the couch watching a *Walking Dead* marathon. On the serious side, you need to ensure you always have safe sex and regular checkups.

Although you've been called inscrutable and deep, that's an illusion caused by the way the light reflects off your marbleized eyes. Of all the signs, yours is the hardest to understand. That's because you have one facial expression—shuttered. Your impossible-to-read look is a definite asset when negotiating a billion-dollar deal (think Bill Gates), but it's not so hot when your lover thinks you've died during sex because you just lie there staring at the ceiling afterward.

Steadfast You

You're Fixed Water. Like a bottomless well, you have a seemingly endless reserve of unconditional love and loyalty. You'll stick by a friend who's in trouble, and make excuses for your kid who stole the minister's car. You'll even stand by a spouse who cheats if you think you can save the relationship. Once you're committed, nothing short of being hit by a bus can make you walk away. And who knows? Maybe even the bus won't stop you.

That's both your gift as well as your downfall. Many astrologers describe you as obtuse as your opposite sign, Fixed-Earth Taurus— and you are. However, your refusal to acknowledge problems is deliberate. No matter how hard you try to pretend, you know what's going on because your ruler, Pluto, is the truth-teller of the universe. Unfortunately for you, it can take most of your life before you admit that you've always known the facts but refused to act on them.

Scorpio lives in the Eighth House of Shared Resources, Sex, and Inheritance. Death is also associated with the eighth house because Pluto was lord of the underworld. But the death associated with the eighth house is tied to the destructive and transformative power of Pluto, and you have the same ability to reinvent yourself and renew your spirit after a crisis. Your courage knows no bounds. You'll tackle any issue, no matter how overwhelming it seems, and usually resolve it. The eighth house is very complex, just like you.

In the eighth house, the soul's connection to others deepens. This area represents what you receive from others. Marriage, long-term relationships, business connections, and physical and emotional inheritances are intertwined. Because Pluto rules this house, power plays within these relationships are highlighted. The eighth house is a financial area and lies opposite the Second House of Money and Values. However, the second house emphasizes "my money," while the eighth house deals with "your or our money." This house represents the person you marry, and what he or she brings to the marriage materially, financially, and spiritually. Nothing is straightforward in this domain.

You may appear quiet or funny or unassuming yet you're deep and moody, and always want control. Pluto operates behind the scenes, digging up secrets. So do you. Although you'll learn everything about everyone who's close to you, not even your best friend will know all about you. Neither will your spouse, which is very handy in case you decide to be bad. You, however, were born with a talent for getting confidential information out of anyone (strangers included), because you know how to keep a confidence. In fact, you collect them.

You're a natural detective, but you don't allow yourself to get close to many people. First, you have to know everything you possibly can about someone, and then you test them. You might pretend to share some confidential information just to see if he or she spreads it around town. Or you may ask for a favor. Winning your trust is like running a marathon: not everyone's up to the challenge.

At work, you're ambitious and flexible. You have a sixth sense about what will work and the unique ability to see opportunities that everyone else misses. You're patient too. You instinctively know exactly the right moment to ask for a raise or apply for a promotion. Although you and your opposite sign, Taurus, share the same determination to succeed, your motives are completely different. Taurus wants money, which equals security. You want power. Even if you're the silent one who pulls the strings behind the scenes, that's okay as long as you're in control.

As a friend, you're devoted and dependable. In love, passionate, and faithful. You're not a social butterfly and prefer your home, family, and a tight circle of longtime friends. Those who are allowed into your inner circle are lucky. When the going gets tough, you know how to get tougher—and where to bury the bodies.

Pluto and You

Until 2024, Pluto in Capricorn is moving through every Scorpio's Third House of Communication. Capricorn represents tradition and power, where Pluto represents transformation and upheaval. During this transit, painful secrets can be revealed. The purpose of Pluto's visit is to teach you to talk to others in a truthful and positive way. This transit can also help you to leave behind any mixed or unpleasant messages about yourself that you received as a child. Read about "The Phoenix of Truth" in part three for a deeper look at some of the challenges and opportunities of Pluto's visit for all Scorpio and Scorpio-rising birthdays.

Sagittarius (November 22–December 21)

Symbol: The Archer
Element: Fire
Quality: Mutable
Polarity: Masculine
Ruler: Jupiter (Zeus)
The Good: Optimistic, playful
The Bad: Tactless, mouthy
The Ugly: Overbearing, commitment phobic

SAGITTARIUS

A Snapshot of Your Sign

Playful, cheerful, and friendly, you're the person everyone else loves to be around. But you're no pushover. Jupiter bestowed both his enthusiasm for life and powerful temper on you. You rarely blow your top. When you do, the blast is over almost as quickly as it started.

The Ninth House of Philosophy, Travel, and Knowledge is home to your larger-than-life soul. You'll talk to anyone about anything and, whether you actually leave home or not, you like to learn about other cultures and countries. Your Mutable-Fire character is comfortable to be around. That's why you're so popular.

Boisterous You

You were born loaded to the eyeballs with BS and equipped with a hair-trigger mouth. Your symbol, the Archer, depicts a centaur (half-man, half-horse being) shooting his arrow of truth into the sky. Sagittarius is known as the dispenser of knowledge, and while that's a noble thought, your idea of knowledge is to babble every random thought that rattles through your head. This excruciating stream of consciousness makes you the biggest windbag in the zodiac—and tactless to boot. Although you don't usually mean to offend anyone, your penchant for talking without thinking first can make you sound super arrogant. Even that kind of verbal hiccupping doesn't stop you, however, because Jupiter, the god who dominated the universe with an unpredictable temper and gift for gab that would choke a Gemini, is your boss.

Jupiter is also responsible for your larger-than-life personality. He's described as a mostly benevolent ruler who liked to meddle in the affairs of both humans and the other gods he bossed around. Jupiter was famous for handing out free advice. You inherited all of his dubious virtues. As soon as an idea hits, it tumbles out of your mouth. And Jupiter's lightning bolts fried those who displeased him. Likewise, your electric zingers leave your friends and family raw from your thoughtless remarks.

Both you and Gemini are Mutable signs. This means that you have the ability to see both sides of an argument, but even so, you can't tolerate opposition. Don't lie to yourself—look at the few close friends you have left. Do they argue with you? Hell no! No one else can speak when you're around because you never take a breath. You attempt to direct every moment of their lives, call them when you need help cleaning your toilet, and order them around with the same enthusiasm as a general ordering troops.

Jupiter is also the god of expansion. That means that you never know how much is enough. Let's say a friend invites twenty guests to her birthday party, you invite a hundred to yours. It doesn't matter that half of them are strangers you rounded up in the parking lot of the local jail. You're concerned with the biggest, not the best. And when your drunken friend falls and breaks his nose, before you call the doctor, you snap a few photos of the bloody mess and post them on your Facebook page.

Jupiter's generous, and so are you—to yourself. To say that you're an impulse buyer is a hilarious understatement. Only a Sagittarius can go to pick up a new pair of shoes and come back with the car stuffed to the roof like a hoarder's house.

You may be the Archer of the universe, but your aim is so far off sometimes that your arrows overshoot your target or fall short of your grandiose promises. You view life through a magnifying glass. For example, no one gets sicker—and to prove it, you'll tweak and poke and chop away at your body to no end, no matter what's really the matter. And no one has more problems. To prove that, you've been known to destroy every relationship you've got. In a nutshell, your arrows are sharp, but you spend most of the time aiming them at your own feet.

Although Sagittarius represents philosophy and deep thinking, you often alienate people with your endless rhetoric. While you think it's a gift, they'll be heading to the nearest ER with a migraine. Oh, and you love sex. In fact, many Sagittarians have a file cabinet full of divorce decrees and/or hate mail to prove it. It's just that your idea of monogamy is having one lover at a time—as in, one lover per encounter. That, and the fact that your attention span is shorter than the nanosecond it takes for you to get your rocks off ensures that your relationships are doomed from the start. But that's okay with you because before you can catch your breath and kick your lover out of bed, you're galloping off in search of your next conquest.

Benevolent You

Yes, you can talk other people into a stupor or rattle their eardrums with your long, loud laugh. On the flip side of your astrological coin, however, no other Sun sign can match your enthusiasm for life. Most astrologers compare Jupiter to the mythic Father Christmas, who was the symbol of cheerful abundance.

Your symbol, Chiron, the centaur, was half-man, half-horse, and all kind-hearted. Although most centaurs were lustful, wild beasts, Chiron, the oldest, was peace loving and wise. He was a tutor to Hercules (or Heracles), who was a friend of Pholus, another unusual centaur known for his kindness and wisdom. During one of his labors (quests), Hercules visited Pholus who offered him shelter and sacred wine, and the vapors from the wine intoxicated the other centaurs. They attacked Hercules, who killed some and drove the rest away. Chiron, who was among them, would neither fight against his herd nor his student. Sadly, as the melee wound down, Hercules mistook Chiron for one of the mean beasts and shot him with a poisoned-tipped arrow. Chiron, being immortal, couldn't die but was in terrible agony. So he told Jupiter, his half-brother, he wanted to give up his immortality to end his pain. Jupiter granted his request but saved him from traveling to Hades by setting him among the stars as the constellation Sagittarius. Jupiter also gave him a bow and arrow to protect the heavens.

You are as generous as Chiron, your symbol, and Pholus, and although you have the adventurous spirit of the other centaurs, your spirit is fun loving and optimistic. Friends can count on you to help in a crisis. You're also the first to volunteer to plan a party. In fact, you love to party so much you'll gladly take over. Of course, this is dangerous for the person footing the bill because it's almost impossible for you to stick to a budget. The good news? You're just as happy to pitch in as much money as you can spare to make the event memorable. You're also as straightforward about asking others to contribute a few bucks, the booze, or the food at your get-togethers.

The Ninth House of Philosophy, Travel, and Knowledge is home to Sagittarius. Here, the soul wants to know more than the next-door gossip associated with the third-house home of Gemini. This soul seeks to learn as much as possible about the world.

You're often described as an adventurer with itchy feet. Although you hate being stuck at home, you aren't necessarily a world traveler. What's important to you is that you're always busy. You're as easily bored as any Air sign, as impatient as your Fiery cousin Aries, and as social as your zodiac opposite, Gemini. Where you run into trouble is thinking that because you like to hear yourself talk, so does everyone else. Take a lesson from Gemini by avoiding socially superficial questions. Patience is not one of your virtues, so listening instead of talking will help you learn how to slow down and understand others.

Slowing down can benefit your health as well. You're one of the most accident-prone signs in the zodiac because your brain is always about three steps ahead of your body. You frequently trip and fall, run into doors, or bang your head because you're not paying attention. Sagittarius rules the hips and thighs, so use caution when you're jogging, exercising, or if you sit at a desk all day. Stand and stretch your spine to avoid lower back problems and take a short walk at lunch or on your break. Overeating is also a danger for you because of your fondness for overindulgence—in food as well as life (another trait you inherited from Jupiter).

You like people, and that genuine affection makes you popular with everyone, from the drunken stranger you let crash on your couch to the neighbors you routinely rescue. Sure, you can meddle in others' lives as much as any Virgo, but you're so damn nice about it that no one minds. Your intent is to help, and you prove it by backing up your advice with action.

Pluto and You

Until 2024, Pluto in Capricorn is moving through every Sagittarius's Second House of Money and Values. Capricorn represents power and tradition, and Pluto rules transformation and upheaval. Watch your budget during this transit because your ability to handle money will be tested. You may experience a financial crisis or find ways to substantially increase your bank account. Your personal value system may also come under scrutiny. Read part three's "Pluto in the Second House" for a deeper look at some of the challenges and opportunities of Pluto's visit for all Sagittarius and Sagittarius-rising birthdays.

Capricorn (December 22–January 19)

Symbol: The Goat
Element: Earth
Quality: Cardinal
Polarity: Feminine
Ruler: Saturn (Cronus)
The Good: Determined, patient
The Bad: Bossy, grumpy
The Ugly: Pretentious, ruthless

CAPRICORN

A Snapshot of Your Sign

Everyone knows you're determined and bossy, and sometimes gloomy. What most people don't know is that you can also be so shy that you feel awkward and out of place even around your best friends.

Saturn is a reclusive planet, and you have a bit of hermit in your soul. Even if you're a Goat that loves to party, you need solitude. You enjoy your own company and can be perfectly content to stay home alone sans text, phone, or internet.

Combining the Tenth House of Career and Public Life and the proactive Cardinal Quality gives you a strong desire to succeed, no matter what you do. Once you focus on a goal, nothing can stop you from reaching it.

Belligerent You

No matter where or to whom you were born, you act as if you were born with a Fortune 100 pedigree. Your ethic is work hard, play harder—oh, and kick any ass that gets in your way. (You can thank your ruling planet, Saturn, for that bit of tough nerve.) Forget fiery Aries and Leo. When it comes to being driven to achieve, no one can compete. Whether breaking the glass ceiling or just crawling out of the gutter, you're determined to climb as high as you can. In fact, you're always on the move—to your next delusion of grandeur—and you don't care who you trample under your little cloven hooves on the way.

You're supposed to have a dry and wickedly funny wit. However, your gags are just that—gag worthy. That often-tasteless banter you call a sense of humor is neither happy nor friendly. One thing about you, though, you're an equal-opportunity offender. You're also known for being gloomy—another trait you inherited from Saturn. The truth is, you have the foulest temper in the zodiac. You don't smile, you grimace. You don't ask, you demand. In case you need to be told, these are some of the reasons why you don't have many friends. Of course, you don't mind. Your massive ego is only outshone by your willingness to suck up to people you despise if they have something you want. Power, money, a cute new lover—you'll do whatever it takes to get them.

Saturn is the god of learning the hard way, and you are his poster child. Your blind will to do everything your way makes stubborn Taurus look like a pushover in comparison. You can be so focused on what you want that you alienate everyone close to you. It's not that you're deliberately callous, it's worse—you hardly ever consider what the other person wants. You expect them to automatically think that whatever you're doing is wonderful. If they sulk, you quit speaking for a week. If they bark back, you bite.

Capricorn is also the sign of reverse aging. This means that, as you age, your disposition gets sweeter until you become a happy, friendly person. The downside? By the time you get playful everyone you know has long since moved on.

Determined You

Capricorn's symbol, the sturdy, sure-footed Goat, fits you perfectly. When you're after something, you never lose sight of your goal, doing whatever it takes to get the prize. The rest of the zodiac can take a lesson from your slow-but-steady progress.

Your legend is connected to Mercury (Hermes), whose affair with a beautiful forest nymph resulted in the birth of Faunus (Pan), the mischievous and well-loved demigod of fields and flocks. Faunus had the upper body of a man and the legs of a goat. When he was born, his mother took one look and bolted, but Mercury adored the little guy and brought him to Mount Olympus, where he became a favorite of the other gods, entertaining them by playing the pipes and dancing. Although Jupiter invited Pan to live on Mount Olympus forever, he declined, preferring to go back to Earth and live in the forest.

Choosing Earth instead of the heavens grounded Pan in more ways than one. Saturn, Capricorn's ruling planet, demands dedication to succeed. There's no free ride with Saturn. However, the rewards of diligence and sweat equity can be amazing. Being born in Saturn's shadow gives you a serious outlook, especially as a child. For some Capricorns, the ability to cut loose and have fun is something one learns to do, not something one's born with.

Capricorn rules the knees and joints. Stress-induced joint pain and knee injuries may have been something you've struggled with since you were a kid. Strengthening your tendons and muscles, and watching your posture so that your joints are properly supported, can be a big help in keeping you flexible and pain free.

Hard work also comes naturally to you because your soul lives in the Tenth House of Career and Public Life, which lies opposite the Fourth House of Home and Family. The tenth-house soul is learning how to put knowledge and skills to useful work that not only benefits you but also the world. The breadwinner figure lives here.

As Cardinal Earth, you instinctively will try to take the lead in everything you do, which isn't always the best course. Although you're devoted to your loved ones, problems arise when you fail to consider letting them in on your ideas before your ideas become decisions you try to force on them. Your opposite sign, Cancer, uses a softer approach that can benefit you. Instead of spouting directives, discuss options. Ask others' opinions. Letting others share the weight relieves the burden of Saturn's philosophy that you always have to bear all the responsibility.

The good news is that, as you age, Faunus's playfulness emerges. You learn how to lighten up and to understand the difference between dictatorship and partnership. When that happens, you begin to relax, and then the real fun starts.

Pluto and You

Until 2024, Pluto in Capricorn is moving through every Capricorn's First House of Self. Capricorn represents status quo and power against Pluto, the planet of transformation and upheaval. The first-house transit is all about asserting your personal power in a positive way. Your self-confidence and self-image undergo changes, and

Pluto can help you to break the power others may have had over you in these areas. You could change your personal style, looks, and gain more confidence in yourself, for example. Read the section on the first house in part three for a deeper look at some of the challenges and opportunities of Pluto's visit for all Capricorn and Capricorn-rising birthdays.

Aquarius (January 20–February 18)

Symbol: The Water Bearer
Element: Air
Quality: Fixed
Polarity: Masculine
Ruler: Uranus (the Greeks called him
   Uranus too) and Saturn (Cronus)
The Good: Nonjudgmental, clever
The Bad: Forgetful, aloof
The Ugly: Sarcastic, unemotional

AQUARIUS

A Snapshot of Your Sign

Rebellious and unpredictable, Uranus rules your sign. Does this automatically make you a capricious rebel? Yes and no. Although you won't hesitate to change jobs or move, or break off a relationship if you see something better that you want, what may look like a sudden change to others is something you've been thinking about for a long, long time.

Your Fixed nature stabilizes your Air Element's tendency to jump first and consider the consequences last. You're the most analytical of all the Air signs, which can make it difficult for you to connect with people on an emotional level. As independent as you can be, Aquarius lives in the Eleventh House of Friends, Groups, and Wishes, which further grounds you. You're an eclectic soul who can move with ease in almost any social circle. Although you may love your family, the bonds of your friendships can be just as tight.

Radical You

Aquarians are born adventurers—that is, if smashing spiders with your bare hands and finding the bathroom in the middle of the night with the lights off count. You love to walk around naked, but naked and drunk is even better. Then you have an excuse for trying to climb through your cute neighbor's bedroom window at 3:00 AM.

You're the zodiac's zone-out sign, but you sure don't mind being weird. In fact, you thrive on being the oddest character around. You look at therapy as a reward for your eccentric behavior because you have a captive audience to listen to the endless recycling of your latest conspiracy theory. And you're as egotistical as your opposite sign, Fixed-Fire Leo. But Leo's ego trips are blatant. She'll flaunt her recent promotion or three-carat diamond in your face. When you feel superior, you shoot your target an all-knowing smirk laced with a touch of pity. Of course, this pisses off your pal, but the more she steams, the more detached you get. Her face reddens, yours goes blank. She raises her voice, you whisper. She rants, you shake your head with concern. If you're lucky enough to wake up in the hospital instead of the morgue, you're genuinely surprised at the wrath you can stir up in other people. Blame Uranus, your ruling planet—and the universe's mad scientist.

Although you're rightly named the zodiac's humanitarian, your compassion can extend so far outward that you can't see what's happening right in front of you. You think you've found a solution for world hunger but don't know how to turn on the stove at home. You fight for human rights but will tell your lover to wear a sack over their head in bed because you're tired of looking at their face, killing both the romance and the relationship. And though you hurt for a couple of days after they leave, you soon forget them and move on.

Abrupt change is part of your life, and most of the time, you initiate the revolution. That's another trait you can thank Uranus for. One day, you awake fed up with your job, your relationship, or your relatives. Sure, your reasons for getting out can be serious, but they're usually only serious to you. Maybe you suddenly decide your boyfriend's worn his favorite shirt once too often, or you can't stand your boss's smile another second. Whatever happens to turn you off happens as fast as flicking a light switch.

You get hot for a cause just as quickly. Then your Fixed-Air flow switches to hurricane force. Of all the talkative Air signs, you're the most obsessive. When you're on a rant, not even Gemini can cut you off. Whether you get a brainstorm about saving the rainforests or decide that red potatoes are toxic, you harangue everyone within earshot with a nonstop stream of chatter. After a few minutes, their eyes glaze, and you're left talking to yourself. But you don't mind because you have all the answers anyway.

Altruistic You

You're the sign of humanity and social conscience, and are interested in making the world a better place. Whether you're volunteering at the local food bank or just listening to your neighbor's latest problems, you do genuinely care about people. Aquarius lives in the Eleventh House of Friends, Groups, and Wishes. That's why you have such a large, eclectic group of acquaintances. Some of your more uptight pals might get occasional culture shock from the variety of characters that come and go in your life, but you have a natural talent for getting along with anyone. Besides, you're curious about human nature and are a natural analyst. Casual labels such as "crazy" or "lazy" or "mean" don't work for you. You want to know why your neighbor lets his family walk all over him. You need to discover the motivation behind your sniping coworker's gossip.

Although your soul's mission is to embrace humanity as a whole, you often appear detached within your closest relationships. You come across as analytical in situations that call for an emotional response. Perhaps your kid bangs up the car. Instead of concentrating on what happened and how to prevent future accidents, it would be better if you concentrated on your kid's feelings first. Stifling your own emotions in a crisis may quell your personal fears while you handle the situation, but walking around with your jaw permanently clenched in an attempt to act rational causes health-harming stress.

Where your body's concerned, Aquarius rules the circulatory system and the ankles. The constant pressure you put on yourself can cause issues with your blood and heart. You may also be prone to swollen legs and ankles from sitting too long at a desk or from lack of exercise. Walking is an excellent activity for you.

Although you're one of the most outspoken signs in the zodiac, your ideas and opinions are aimed at improving a situation. You spend a lot of your time thinking of solutions and never have any trouble handing out advice. At your best, you say what's on your mind then step out of the picture—unless you're asked to help further or you're trying to win an argument with someone close. Then you have the tendency to hold the anger and the stress it causes way too long.

Take a lesson from your opposite sign, Leo. The fifth house, where Leo lives, is full of passion, fun, and romance. Spontaneous, cheerful Leo rarely broods over anything. Leo's Fixed Fire burns bright and hot, and she can yell as loud as any Aries. Nevertheless, once the feud is settled, Leo moves on. Leos concentrate on what makes them happy. You tend to keep rehashing the situation long after everyone else has forgotten what the fight was about. Instead of wasting energy thinking up new arguments to old squabbles, do something that makes you feel good. Dive into the internet for an hour and check out the latest conspiracy theories. Or visit your favorite bistro and people watch. Getting your mind off a situation you can't change lessens your stress and brings your focus back to your physical and mental health, where it belongs.

Radical Uranus gives you the ability to revise your life or alter your course at any time. Uranus dislikes restraint and conformity—that's why you seem to be automatically against anything that's too traditional. However, you're also ruled by Saturn, the planet of discipline and hard work. Add your Fixed-Air Quality, and that explains why you get obsessive about having others follow your advice. This mix also makes you both a visionary and an ass kicker.

Your symbol, the Water Bearer, is one of the oldest constellations and, as such, has some varied stories of how it came to be. One of the most common is associated with Ganymede, a sexy young man whom Jupiter abducted to be his lover at Mount Olympus. Jupiter also made Ganymede immortal—eternally young—and declared him to be the official cupbearer to the gods there, replacing his daughter Juventas (Hebe), who'd previously held the position. Promotions aside, Jupiter's wife, Juno (Hera), was not pleased, and Jupiter eventually resolved it by placing Ganymede in the sky as the constellation Aquarius—the Water Bearer—to oversee the entire water supply of the world. Aquarius was associated with the annual flooding of the Nile, for example, which brought life-giving water to the farms that bordered the great river.

In modern times, the Water Bearer is associated with the Age of Aquarius, when the good of all humanity will prevail over the few who would dictate to the masses how they should live their lives. The "water" that Aquarius pours on the Earth is knowledge and enlightenment.

Pluto and You

Until 2024, Pluto in Capricorn is moving through every Aquarian's Twelfth House of Secrets, Illusion, and the Subconscious. Capricorn represents power, and Pluto is the planet of transformation. What secrets still hold power over your life? Self-deceit is one of the nastiest traps in this abode. This is another one of the harsher Pluto transits because the twelfth house contains the subconscious mind and all the hurtful secrets it holds.

At the same time, this transit has the greatest power to bring spiritual peace. This transit can help you learn to accept your flaws as well as the flaws of others. Read the last section in part three—"Pluto in the Twelfth House: The Phoenix of Acceptance"—for a deeper look at some of the challenges and opportunities of Pluto's visit for all Aquarius and Aquarius-rising birthdays.

PISCES

Pisces (February 19–March 20)

Symbol: The Fishes
Element: Water
Quality: Mutable
Polarity: Feminine
Ruling planet: Neptune (Poseidon)
The Good: Empathetic, forgiving
The Bad: Indecisive, lazy
The Ugly: Escapist, oversensitive

A Snapshot of Your Sign

As the last sign of the zodiac, you have a great empathy for the eleven souls that came before you. According to the reincarnation theory, you've lived in their shoes and have retained a bit of each one's traits.

Whether you believe you were once an Aries or Libra, or any of the other signs, you can't deny that you're able to identify with what others are feeling—or even read their minds. Your Mutable Water picks up emotional vibrations like a cell phone picks up electromagnetic waves from the tower.

The Twelfth House of Secrets, Illusion, and the Subconscious is home to Pisces, which deepens your ability to tap into other people's heads. The Fishes of your symbol are usually depicted as being bound with a silver cord, with one fish swimming up and one swimming down. Far from the everyday explanation that you are always struggling to stay afloat in life, the true meaning is that you are connected to both this world and the next.

Spacy You

Like the Wizard of Oz, you operate behind a curtain of illusion. One minute you're impressing powerful people with your initiative and the next you're refusing to answer the door when opportunity tries to kick it down.

Instead of grabbing the big breaks that appear, you wave from the sidelines as they pass. Then you spend the next ten years imagining what you could have had—the perfect lover, the fabulous career, the limitless income. In reality, many Pisces tend to marry a string of losers, hop from one dead-end job to another, and never have enough money to pay the bills.

Too bad you weren't born with spiny barbs all over your skin—then it wouldn't hurt so much when others wipe their feet on you. Although you can be fearsome when it comes to protecting a loved one, the thought of standing up for yourself is as foreign to you as being faithful is to a Sagittarian. If you didn't have a fantasy life, you'd have no life at all.

As a fence-straddling Pisces, you'd rather be pushed into oncoming traffic than take a risk. You may spout that you're afraid of losing everything you've built for yourself (that one change of clothing and the three cold beers you own), but you know the truth. Responsibility—you can't handle it. Oh sure, you can sit in the ER all night for a sick friend, work three or four dead-end jobs to support your sixth chronically unemployed partner, and move old Aunt May into the spare bedroom, thinking you're being noble—and maybe you are. Then again, maybe the selfless image you show to the world is only a smokescreen.

You're a Water sign like Cancer and Scorpio. However, Cancer the Crab can live on the beach and Scorpio's Scorpion can survive in the desert. You're all Water, and water always seeks the lowest level. If you're always stuck in an emotional bog, then you never have to raise your eyes higher than the swamp. Of course, that's okay with you—taking responsibility for everyone else keeps you from taking responsibility for yourself. Besides, you love to complain about what you could have accomplished if only you hadn't been tied down. Your list of excuses is endless, and the sad thing is that you believe every one of them. Self-deceit is one of your strongest traits. You can thank Neptune, the gasbag planet of illusion, for that talent.

In all honesty, you really can't help deluding yourself. Pisces's home on the zodiac wheel is the twelfth house. Illusion, self-undoing, hidden enemies—it's a nasty place to live, but you handle it well. And when you're not playing doormat for the world, you're playing around. But somebody always betrays you in the end, and you can't blame them, you ask for it every time. Secretly, you liked being dumped. When your dreamboats sink back into the mud you hauled them out of, you have an excuse to drown in self-pity.

You're also the most forgetful sign on the planet. Only Pisces can head to the grocery store and end up being stopped for speeding forty miles out of town. And you'll have no idea how you got there because the second you put the key in the ignition, you blanked out of reality and into one of your pipe dreams.

When it comes to planning ahead, you're as bad as your opposite sign, Virgo—not because you are addicted to details but because you never remember them. You put the date for your best friend's birthday on your calendar then forget to plan the party. By the time you think to visit Granny in the hospital, she's in the ground. But that's no problem because you're also telepathic. So you just go home and have a private séance with her. All you need is a candle and that bottle of Thunderbird you've been saving for a special occasion.

Soulful You

You're the last sign of the zodiac, and your soul contains the collective traits of each of the eleven signs before you—the reason you're so empathetic. You truly can walk in someone else's shoes and feel what they feel.

Feelings define you. And if you aren't careful, you can emotionally drown because you absorb the mood of the moment. Instead of separating yourself from the heat, you go on autopilot and nod assent without taking the time to think. Later, when you're alone, you often reassess the situation and come up with a very different view.

Once you learn how to pause before you unconsciously agree with the crowd, you'll save yourself a lot of trouble. (That reflexive action is where you got your reputation for being a pushover.) You know how to say no. You just need to learn how to stop being fearful of being rejected if you give your true opinion. A Pisces soul wants to please everyone, but in the real world, you lose yourself by trying to make everyone else happy—you explode just like Neptune, your ruling planet.

Neptune (Poseidon) was the god of the sea—all waters—and brother to Jupiter (Zeus) and Pluto (Hades). These three conquered their father, Saturn (Cronus), and divided his kingdom. Although mostly peaceful, Neptune had an ugly temper that caused great storms and violence on the surface of the sea. His unpredictable anger made everyone who lived on the coast afraid of him, though he was also responsible for calm waters and the granting of safe passage. No one knew what made him mad, so they tiptoed around, anxious and fearful.

Like the ocean, you may look and act calm on the outside when you're actually churning on the inside. Sooner or later, your goldfish nature turns into shark-bite anger that causes the same reactions in your friends and family as in the residents on the shores of Neptune's seas. Learning to control the chaos inside you will help to keep you on an even keel.

Virgo, your opposite sign, resides in the Sixth House of Everyday Work, Service, and Health. This Mutable-Earth sign also gets very involved in other people's lives. However, Virgo's Earth Element bestows a more practical nature. Virgo rarely agrees with anything before giving it careful consideration. Even a trip to the corner store can turn into a logistics nightmare because Virgo has to have every detail mapped out in advance.

But when you tap into Virgo's methodical energy, you calm down. The slower pace of pausing for a few seconds to be mindful helps you to clear your head. When you do that, you can look at any issue much more objectively. Walking also helps you to eliminate stress. Pisces rules the feet, and keeping them and your body in motion gets you out of your own head so that you can absorb the good energy of the outdoors. Dancing is another way to work off your angst.

As mentioned earlier, the Pisces symbol of the Fishes is usually depicted as two fish swimming in opposite directions but bound together with a cord. Their struggle represents the internal war you wage between living in the real world and escaping your problems via the fantasies in your head. Although this representation is what most astrologers use, the more accurate version is the story of Venus, Cupid, and the Typhon.

The Typhon was known as the Father of All Monsters—a monster so horrible he even terrified the gods. When he decided to attack Mount Olympus, the gods fled. Venus (Aphrodite) and her son, Cupid (Eros), got cut off from the others and ended up on the shore of the Euphrates, with no way to escape. Two fish appeared and offered to take Venus and Cupid across the river. They let her lash them together with a golden cord so they wouldn't get separated, and she and Cupid rode on their backs to safety. As a reward for their courage, she honored the fish by placing them among the stars as the constellation Pisces. A modern twist on this tale suggests that the fish are actually dolphins, because they are intelligent, friendly to humans, and seem to have the desire to communicate with us.

Like the friendly dolphins, you strive to understand everyone you meet. You walk with one foot on the Earth and the other tied to the heavens. You have a soul-deep need to rescue people, making you the person strangers approach to spill their troubles to.

Though you're versatile and receptive, you thrive when you allow yourself periods of solitude. Being alone clears your heart and your head. Privacy also helps you to unlock your creative energy, which can be a direct conduit from the universe to the world. When you learn to focus your imagination and develop your sense of self (versus self-sacrifice), you'll transform into an unstoppable force of nature.

Pluto and You

Until 2024, Pluto in Capricorn is moving through every Pisces's Eleventh House of Friends, Groups, and Wishes. Capricorn represents tradition and power, and Pluto is the planet of transformation. You may gain some rich and powerful benefactors. You may choose to eliminate some dysfunctional friendships. Chances are you'll meet a few people who have different lifestyles than yours, so you might have to reassess your role within your friendships or the groups to which you belong. But don't be afraid. Instead, embrace these new experiences as chances to learn a thing or two about yourself along the way. Read the section on the eleventh house in part three for a deeper look at some of the challenges and opportunities of Pluto's visit for all Pisces and Pisces-rising birthdays.

Now that you've had the opportunity to dig into your Sun sign and take a peek into how Pluto-in-Capricorn's influence in your life might play out over the coming years, it's time to get up close and personal. Grab some Dramamine—when Pluto's throwing his weight around your house, things can get bumpy. Luckily, if you keep your wits and choose to meet him head on, you can transform Pluto's curveballs into a positive force of change in every area of your life.

PART THREE

Pluto and the Houses

You've taken the long view of Pluto in Capricorn in the generations, and experienced the tighter focus of his clout on your Sun sign and rising sign. Now, it's time to crank that telescopic lens to Pluto-in-your-face intensity.

Remember, Capricorn is the sign of tradition, power plays, and control. Ruled by heavy-handed Saturn, Capricorn wants to be absolute ruler. Pluto is the disrupter. He agitates the status quo, shreds the cover-ups, and exposes misconceptions—even lies—that have influenced what you believe about yourself and your life. Life is a journey full of plot twists, emotional upheavals, and amazing surprises. Pluto's trip through your soul is no different. Ideally, as the soul travels through the various signs and houses around the zodiac wheel, it learns the lesson of each house and grows spiritually. But as souls are connected to humans and all humans are flawed and frail, we need time to recognize the issues, reorganize our thought patterns, and rid ourselves of negative behaviors. In the houses of your personal astrology chart, Pluto's powerful force works in two very significant ways: natal Pluto and transit Pluto.

Extracting Pluto's Diamonds

First, most of us will only live through six or seven Pluto transits during our lifetime. This means that the house—or life area—of your natal chart that Pluto occupied the day you were born has special significance to your personal evolution. Natal Pluto issues are usually played out by your parents or caregivers, but you absorb these energy patterns from the moment you're born. Whether negative or positive, the examples your family set are permanent, becoming part of your character. These issues are special to you and your spiritual growth, and they represent both lifelong challenges and your deepest strengths. Whatever house Pluto occupies in your natal chart reflects the childhood imprinting of that house's themes.

Second, as Pluto moves through the houses of your chart, he activates the issues of the house he's transiting. These long, slow journeys are complicated and, at times, feel like karmic payback—but they serve the purpose of helping you to make permanent and positive changes.

During these visits, he uncovers patterns of dysfunction and codependency you might still be living with or covering up. He exposes issues you've hidden or ignored and digs up the skeletons you've tried to bury. Oh sure, you can choose to bury them again, but he'll just keep digging until everything falls apart, sometimes through an illness, loss, or a sudden shock. You can't prevent experiencing pain and grief, but you can choose to heal.

Pluto's job is to help you to recognize where you're on autopilot and repeating self-defeating patterns. To accomplish that, he leans on you until you squeal. Ignore him, and the pressure builds until you're forced to deal with a crisis. Or perhaps you meet another cute loser, you find another dead-end job, you get verbally abused by another bully. Not all Pluto tests are as harsh. However, all do reveal where you most resist change. The good news is that you also receive new opportunities for success. As you become mindful, you'll move beyond the past and learn how to make better choices that help you reframe your life in a positive way.

Although you'll get pushed to the wall with Pluto in residence, you'll also discover—and learn how to use—the hidden strengths and power he brings to that area of your life.

Traps and Hidden Treasures

In the 1959 Twentieth Century Fox film *Journey to the Center of the Earth*, a group of explorers goes on an expedition to discover the heart of the planet. On the way, they find paths that lead to dead ends, they suffer earthquakes and rockslides, and they meet monsters. They also discover a cavern full of precious gems, and life-saving water and food. When they finally reach the center of Earth, they build a raft and sail away, only to be sucked into one last deadly vortex before they climb into a fireproof altar stone and are shot back to the surface and safety via an erupting volcano.

Sounds like your average Pluto transit.

There's no easy way through the journey to the deepest part of your soul, and no way to avoid facing some nasty truths. Each trip usually starts with a jolt. An issue from your past resurfaces, a suppressed memory bubbles up, someone you thought was long gone reappears. By the time the shock settles a bit, you might feel as if you've been singled out for some cosmic bashing, but in order to break those unconscious patterns, you must first be aware you have them. Pluto makes sure that you do. If you're the kind of person who learns the first time, you're not only rare, you're lucky.

Most of us have to be hit over the head a few times before we really start to pay attention to what Pluto's trying to tell us—and some of us never learn. Those are the people who go through life constantly complaining about how hard they have it, never realizing their attitudes and actions have attracted most of their angst. The faster you can make yourself aware of your negative habits, the easier your Pluto journey will be.

Surviving a Pluto transit takes guts. It might even take therapy. This slow process starts with you being mindful of what's really going on in your life. Are you being reminded of past actions that you refused to change? Maybe you gossiped about someone who's now in a position to help or hurt you. Are you treating every new love like the one dirtbag who broke your heart? Perhaps you're hanging on to old hurts and grief that prevent your happiness. As long as you cling to the painful part of your life, you hand control of your future to those who have hurt you. The good news is that you already have the tools you need to succeed—you were born with them. Now, you're going to learn how to use them.

Riding the Volcano Back Into the Sunshine

If you work on your issues, the speed bumps during a Pluto transit can be smaller. If you don't, you may feel like you've smashed into a tree at eighty miles an hour. Want revenge? Avoiding the truth? Feel like your world is crashing? He doesn't care. His job is to make you aware of it. Your job is to deal with it. And when you do, he morphs from bully to bodyguard and gives you the courage to make the changes that can save you.

The truths he churns up can be brutal, but ignoring them will only cause you further pain, clouding every future choice you make. Most crucially, refusing to acknowledge them prevents you from receiving the happiness you deserve and evolving on a spiritual level. When Pluto passes through a house, any or all of the themes in that life area are brought to the surface, either to be transformed or demolished.

Pluto's here to make your soul evolve and to destroy anything that prevents you from growing into the person you were meant to be. No one is immune. We all have less-than-stellar behaviors—we're greedy or needy or nasty. We cheat. We lie. We neglect our health. We wallow in self-pity. It's easy to take the low road, as anger is easier to express than forgiveness. And blame is easier to put on the other person.

We learn most of these damaging behaviors in childhood, which is why you'll see numerous references in the following sections to parents, caregivers, and other authority figures. Messages we received from these power figures are expressed through the unconscious behavior patterns and self-perceptions that color every situation and relationship in our lives. How we express this energy depends upon the house that Pluto was in at birth or is currently transiting.

When you burn your finger, you're instantly aware of the physical pain. Pluto transits teach you how to become aware of the psychological patterns that cause emotional pain. Recycling the behaviors that hold you down is as crazy as sticking your hand in a fireplace. But if you begin boosting your awareness now, you can emerge this

Pluto transit stronger, wiser, and more in control of your life than you've ever been. When you walk in awareness, you're ready for whatever life hands you, you discover how to create a better life than the one determined by your past.

Facing your demons through a Pluto transit isn't for sissies. Pluto shatters the subconscious structures that have prevented your growth. And like a codependent in a dysfunctional family, you cling to the things that keep you trapped. As he pushes you toward the truth, you may crumble. You may stumble through that dark tunnel as he blocks the light at the other end. The more work you need to do, the worse this trip can be. However, if you keep pushing through the darkness, you will find your inner strength. That's when you'll discover the other side of his potent force.

Pluto rules the energy that gives you the courage to transform your life—he helps you turn a trap into a trapdoor of escape. Choosing to be true to you is tough. You have to be willing to break from unhealthy relationships and lose some bad habits. You have to admit some disagreeable things about yourself. In the process, you'll also learn there's nothing you've suffered that you can't overcome. There's nothing you've done that's so bad that you can't find self-forgiveness. And when you do, you'll find redemption.

A Spin Around the Zodiac

As we discussed in "Five Ways to Gain and Grow with Pluto" in the introduction, your natal chart is based on the exact moment of your birth. This pie-shaped chart is divided into twelve sections, or houses, and these twelve houses of the horoscope roughly correspond with the stages of life and, on a karmic level, the soul's journey around this eternal hamster wheel. The houses are where you and Pluto meet face to face—where you'll have to take on his challenges in order to find your inner treasures.

As in the Sun sign section (part two) we use the Roman names of the gods and goddesses that roam through the houses. You can find their Greek equivalents in the "Quick Guide to Roman Gods and Other Mythological People and Creatures" table on page 215. In this last part of the book (part three), each individual house chapter begins with a short introduction that will act as a tour of that area, helping you to understand a bit about the primary traits and basic influences associated with that space before you dig in. Imagine taking a drive through the different neighborhoods in your town. If you observe the homes you pass, you can learn a few things about the folks who live in them.

Keep in mind that the energy, strengths, and challenges of each house are different. When Pluto moves in, he churns up anything that needs fixing. Pluto is working in several areas of your life at once. The natal and transiting houses are the most important, but for a deeper and more global look at your life, also read about the houses that affect your Sun sign and rising sign. (Checking your natal chart before you begin this section would be beneficial.)

Ready for your close-up?

HOUSE	WITH PLUTO	SIGN (& SYMBOL)	RULING PLANET	CHARACTERISTICS
First House of Self	Phoenix of Identity (Be true to yourself, and achieve your best, inside and out)	Aries (The Ram) ♈	Mars (Warrior and hero)	Action-driven, Enthusiastic, Impatient, Hot-tempered Body Area: the head
Second House of Money and Values	Phoenix of Values (Cultivate your financial and moral resources)	Taurus (The Bull) ♉	Venus (Lover of people and worldly comforts)	Security-driven, Loyal, Generous, Judgmental Body Areas: the throat and neck
Third House of Communication	Phoenix of Truth (Find your true voice)	Gemini (The Twins) ♊	Mercury (Curious messenger)	Curious, Sociable, Gossipy, Intellectual Body Areas: the nervous system, lungs, arms, and hands
Fourth House of Home and Family	Phoenix of Nurturing (Create a safe environment and loving family)	Cancer (The Crab) ♋	The Moon (Elusive nurturer)	Caring, Manipulative, Strong-willed, Sensitive Body Areas: the breasts, stomach, and upper digestive tract
Fifth House of Creativity, Children, and Romance	Phoenix of Creativity (Release your inhibition to discover your natural talents)	Leo (The Lion) ♌	The Sun (Center of the solar system and lifegiver)	Courageous, Kind-hearted, Overbearing, Faithful Body Areas: heart and back
Sixth House of Everyday Work, Service, and Health	Phoenix of Service (Balance your health and daily routine)	Virgo (The Virgin) ♍	Mercury (Detailed communicator)	Analytical, Helpful, Restless, Hypercritical Body Areas: the nervous system and lower digestive tract

HOUSE	WITH PLUTO	SIGN (& SYMBOL)	RULING PLANET	CHARACTERISTICS
Seventh House of Partnership	Phoenix of Partnership (Achieve harmonious relationships)	Libra (The Scales of Justice) ♎	Venus (Fair-minded peacekeeper)	Objective, Narcissistic, Negotiator, Agreeable Body Areas: the kidneys and lower back
Eighth House of Shared Resources, Sex, and Inheritance	Phoenix of Legacy (Cultivate emotional legacy with others)	Scorpio (The Scorpion) ♏	Pluto (Transformative disrupter) Mars (Passionate protector)	Supportive, Devoted, Private, Vengeful Body Area: the reproductive organs
Ninth House of Philosophy, Travel, and Knowledge	Phoenix of Belief (Explore lifelong learning for the collective good)	Sagittarius (The Archer) ♐	Jupiter (Bossy benefactor)	Optimistic, Playful, Commitment-phobic, Long-winded Body Areas: the hips and thighs
Tenth House of Career and Public Life	Phoenix of Integrity (Align personal truth with public truth)	Capricorn (The Goat) ♑	Saturn (Demanding taskmaster)	Patient, Determined, Dedicated, Ruthless Body Areas: the knees and joints
Eleventh House of Friends, Groups, and Wishes	Phoenix of Revolution (Expand social consciousness for greater freedom)	Aquarius (The Water Bearer) ♒	Uranus (Eclectic revolutionary and humanitarian) Saturn (Stern traditionalist)	Nonjudgmental, Nonconformist, Sarcastic, Inventive Body Areas: the circulatory system and ankles
Twelfth House of Secrets, Illusion, and the Subconscious	Phoenix of Acceptance (Release past negative patterns to evolve spiritually)	Pisces (The Fishes) ♓	Neptune (Passionate illusionist)	Visionary, Empathetic, Intuitive, Escapist Body Area: the feet

PLUTO IN THE FIRST HOUSE

The Phoenix of Identity

At a Glance: The First House

Who are you? This hall of mirrors is all about the self. It's where the zodiac and the soul begin. The Ascendant, or rising sign, is also here. The first house is the outward face we show to the world—that surface personality we project and the first impression we make on others. Just as a baby is preoccupied with his own fingers and toes, this home relates to the world as it revolves around the owner.

Remove the Mask

Because the first house contains your self-image and identity, the good news is that this transit is all about you. What's the bad news? Some days, you're not going to know who's Dr. Jekyll and who's Mr. Hyde. You or the people who helped form your self-image? Both.

The first house on your natal chart is where you find your Ascendant (rising sign). One trait of the first house is to act as a buffer between you and the rest of the world—the prepackaged personality you present when interacting with others. Both the first impression you make on others and your initial impression of them are filtered through the Ascendant. Suppose someone bad-mouths you. A slew of emotions may run through your head. You're furious. Or humiliated. Or amused. One of these feelings will trigger an auto-response. Will you shrug it off or go for the throat? Do others think you're bossy and critical? Or are you the reliable one who keeps everyone else together (but has no one to lean on but yourself)? *Who are you?* That's the big question you're asked to investigate, because what you don't realize is that much of what you think are instinctive behaviors are actually learned responses to your childhood environment.

Although the face you show to the world may have a big grin plastered on it, when Pluto begins pecking under your skin that carefully crafted smile starts to crack. Hidden behind this facade are long-buried misrepresentations, and one of the purposes of this trip is to scrape off the superficial behaviors that have blocked the best traits of who you are deep inside. Maybe you had a turbulent relationship with one of your parents, you learned to argue at a very early age, or your voice was lost in the family chaos. Perhaps your plan to have a career clashed with the family tradition. Whatever the circumstances, the survival mechanisms you developed to cope are all jumbled up with the primary characteristics of your rising sign.

Identity Crisis

As a baby, you didn't understand the concept that you were a separate being apart from your parents. Later, you knew you were independent from them, but that didn't mean you grew up to be self-empowered. Now that Pluto's digging around in your first house, you have to sort through a lot of garbage to get to the *real* you. This trip can be a radical journey that puts you on an emotional teeter-totter. The more clutter you need to clear, the longer you'll bounce up and down.

In the first house, Pluto's aim is to force you to recognize the deceptive patterns that have masked who you are deep inside. To do that, he pushes the repeat button on behaviors that poke at your self-image. This irritates the fiery Mars energy that rules the first house and ratchets your irritability factor. You can become annoyed with others' behaviors that you previously overlooked or made excuses for. You also may kick yourself over traits you've always had that begin to feel phony or weak. Even if you're naturally an independent spirit, you will most likely demand more freedom. That's one side of the teeter-totter.

The other side of the teeter-totter holds an instinctive need to be wanted, also a first-house trait. Aries, the sign that influences this house, has many childlike qualities and fears abandonment. Although Aries is Masculine Cardinal Fire, a force that's both dominant and domineering, this energy is that of a baby crying when it's hungry, wet, or tired.

When Pluto steps across the threshold, he stirs up your desire to understand who you are, separate from everyone else, and you begin to struggle with the image that was created for you in childhood. At the same time, you may be uncomfortable making waves. Stepping out of the shadow of your family or away from people who may have manipulated your behavior through the years causes repercussions. Some people can't cope with the changes you make. Others think you're abandoning them, or they are offended because you dare to be your own person.

First-house energy is hotheaded and impulsive, so don't be surprised if you develop a very thin skin during this transit. You can meditate, medicate, or bury your head in the sand for years, trying to avoid the increasing tension, but unless you meet it head on, sooner or later, you'll explode.

Boiling Point

Every house has an opposite on the zodiac wheel. The first house of *me* is opposite the seventh house of *we*. Libra, the sign of balance, lives in the Seventh House of Partnerships. Venus rules this house, and the themes are harmony and fair play.

Mars, the warrior planet, commands the first house. Aries, the Ram, lives here. This home is self-focused. *I come first. I want my way.* When Pluto steps over the threshold, independence becomes more important than ever. In fact, it can become an obsession, especially if other people have had too much power over you.

Mars isn't introspective. He demands self-expression and action. When angry, he's the guy who throws the first punch. Pluto's a moody recluse—and sneaky too. Instead of punching your lights out, he turns the lights out and then pushes you down the stairs. When these two collide, you can expect to experience some serious internal conflict. Dr. Mars Jekyll wants to win. Mr. Pluto Hyde wants control. Mars says, "As long as I get my way, we'll get along." Pluto replies, "I don't care if we get along. Don't get in my way." Neither is right. Mars's anger flares then fizzles where Pluto's anger is caustic, and both can cause lasting damage. When Pluto stirs up your deepest needs to be yourself, it's bound to cause turmoil within your tightest relationships.

Identity struggles are common in the first house. Issues you've tried to forget or prided yourself on overcoming return like that bum of a family member asking for another loan. If you have overcome them, that's great, this transit will be easier on you. If you've buried them, prepare to dance with the bones of your past.

The flip side of trying to find your backbone is twisting Pluto's muscle and Mars's hair-trigger temper into Mr. Hyde's meanness.

Born with Pluto in her first house, Jane radiated intensity. The impression she made was that of an overconfident super snob with a chip on her shoulder the size of Alaska. Although being rejected was her worst fear, her thorny personality and unpredictable temper ruined her relationships, including her marriage. After years of enduring her verbal abuse, her husband walked out. And Jane reeled from the shock. That's Pluto's zero-tolerance policy at work—Jane was out of control and he steered her into a brick wall. Jane had to face a blast of negative blowback to finally see the damage she'd caused. In a panic, she begged her husband for another chance, and they started couples therapy. The journey hasn't been easy, but they are back together and making steady progress.

Of course, this natal placement doesn't automatically condemn you to a life of hostility, but it does bestow you with a powerful personality. Think of Hillary Clinton and His Holiness the Dalai Lama, both born with Pluto in the first house. Though your life might not play out on the world stage, you were given this inner strength to make a positive impact in your personal world. The key is to strive to avoid walking around with your hackles up like an angry cat, viewing life as a never-ending battle.

Self-Defense

Pluto earned his reputation as a cold-blooded recluse who couldn't have cared less about the souls he delivered into Hades. When you think about how he was treated—first by his father, Saturn, who swallowed him, then his shady brothers, Neptune and Jupiter, who probably swindled him—it's easier to understand why he's such a hard-ass. When he blows into your first house, the wind gusting in with him is more icy blast from the past than fresh spring breeze. He dredges up issues that have made you feel helpless, then he hammers you with repeat scenarios until, hopefully, you recognize the pattern. The purpose is to toughen you up enough to be your best self, not who someone else wants you to be.

Stuck in doormat mode? Say hello to more feet that will be thrilled to wipe their shoes on you. Have you put your partner in the position of being the stable parent you never had? Get ready to be bossed around like a three-year-old. You could have grown up thinking that you weren't good enough, smart enough, or attractive enough. Maybe you were brainwashed concerning sexual stereotypes—men must be macho, women should be helpless. Clichés? Sure. But every bit of information you received as a child affects the way you present yourself now.

Perhaps your parents demanded that you always be polite, no exceptions. Once you grew up, your logical mind agreed that it wasn't nice to wipe your mouth on your sleeve or drop the f-bomb around born-again Aunt Gladys. However, your unconscious never moved beyond the no-exceptions rule. It interpreted that rule to include being polite to everyone, even to people who really needed a swift kick in the butt. To compensate for years of shrugging off others' bad behaviors, you got the wrong idea that you're an easygoing diplomat. What you really are is someone who can't tell the difference between having manners and allowing others to walk all over you.

In this case, Pluto's intention is to get you to stand up for your-self. Your soul can't evolve when you're living in a fog. You must be conscious of what's going on around you. Sounds like no-brainer advice, doesn't it? But chances are you spend a huge amount of your lifetime walking around on autopilot. Do you have the same arguments with the same people over the same issues and nothing's ever resolved? Think about your motives. Are you afraid they won't like you? And if they don't, would that be bad? Although fear of rejection is a first-house trait, Mars demands action. With Pluto egging on the warrior inside you, the need to break free can become extreme. You must shed both the people and the behaviors that hold you back. Nothing will change unless you do.

Another path is the one that brings you face to face with the beast in the mirror. As in Jane's case, all of the hostility you've turned on others can come back to bite you. Or you could get paralyzed by your own anger, as Ethan did.

Ethan was the youngest member of the writers' critique group he attended with his father. At sixteen, he was a better writer than his father, who still struggled with a novel he'd started fifteen years before. Several years later, and despite a promising career, larger success didn't come because Ethan's seething anger had imploded.

When Pluto prodded Ethan to create his own identity, he couldn't break away from his family patterns. Instead of separating himself from his dad, he took his father's failure on his shoulders. Out of guilt, Ethan tried to live his father's dream but continually shot himself in the foot with self-sabotage. Like Pluto, Ethan struggled with his relationship with his father—he wanted to be a good son, but he did not want to be a writer. His conflicting emotions eventually turned into battles of will with everyone, from his dad to his mentor to the friends he'd made in his writers' group. His struggle ended when he found the courage to speak the truth and step out of his father's shadow. When Ethan separated himself from his father's dream, he found his own path and followed it. He's now enrolled in college and studying to be an architect.

What kind of identity struggles have you had that you can reflect on in your life? Is your identity your own or one that's been thrust upon you? Have you been playing a role that someone else defined for you? Only *you* can define who you are. Tension and anger always surface during the first-house transit, and you shouldn't suppress it—but beware. Using Pluto's power to fuel personal revenge will only get you in a tornado of trouble. Stop and think before you act. As harsh as Pluto's lessons can be, if you work with him, he'll teach you how to redefine your image and protect you from those who could harm you—including yourself.

Power Plays

During a first-house transit, you're getting guidance in how to use the power of your rising sign (personality) in a way that enhances the strengths of your Sun sign (character). To accomplish that, Pluto stirs up primal survival instincts. Suddenly, you may find that you can't stand anything that smacks of control. It may be as minor as being annoyed by your sister's habit of dropping by without calling first or as major as a volcanic-force eruption of the long-simmering anger in your marriage.

Self-defense is a normal human reaction. However, with Pluto prodding you in the first house, you may be overly defensive because you've instinctively become aware of the deceptive behaviors that have stifled you. Although you must express what you truly feel in order to grow, you must also be mindful about how you communicate. Argue for your rights. Be as hardnosed as you want, but fight fair. If you feel rage building, try to work it off before you erupt. Physical activities that make you sweat and temporarily forget can help. Or vent to a friend—but don't make it an hours-long whine fest. You can't run away from these unresolved issues. Trying to flee them is like riding a merry-go-round. You may be moving but you're only going around in circles. Until you jump off, you'll never go anywhere.

Be Your Best, Inside and Out

The first house is one of your health areas, and actions you take during this transit have long-lasting results. Your self-image lives here, and part of that concept is your appearance. When Pluto moves in, he drags a full-length mirror with him. Why would this reclusive and introverted character care about how you look? He doesn't. Pluto isn't your personal stylist. He rules things that are hidden, bringing up issues that you've accepted as something you must live with, and then he helps you to change them. Included in the mix can be concerns about the way you look, and self-esteem about one's appearance is fragile. Everyone understands how harmful a single word or disapproving glance can be.

Maybe you inherited your great-grandfather's hump of a nose, and you hate it. Or you're beginning to look too much like one of your parents. You may or may not hate this, but you aren't ready to see your mother's face or your father's chin peering back at you in the mirror. Much of the transformation during this period can be as minor as changing your hair color. Or maybe you lose weight because the rustling sound of your chaffed thighs rubbing together starts grating on your ears.

This Pluto transit helps you learn that you don't have to be stuck with what you don't like about yourself. But it's an ongoing process, and you have time to tweak and readjust—to try on different images. These are the years to develop your personal sense of style and to learn how to create the best image for you.

Jeannie's nose looked like the description of great-granddad's above. However, her self-image was bolstered by a family who praised her special beauty, helping her to survive the inevitable schoolyard insults. Her large, almond-shaped eyes and flawless complexion added to her good looks. Today, she wouldn't think of altering her appearance into what she describes as "a bland, blonde clone." That's her opinion, and thanks to the supportive message she received from her family, when her Pluto test came, she didn't cave in to the pressure to look like everyone else.

Does that mean you shouldn't have a nip and tuck if you want one? Of course not. But this transit isn't about being stuck with what you don't like or discarding who you are. It's about reinforcing the best in you instead of trying to mold yourself into a preconceived definition of healthy or sexy or beautiful. *Your* choice is what counts.

Because the first house is all about action, this transit emphasizes physical exercise that keeps your body in shape. If you're open to this dynamic energy force, Pluto the personal trainer will kick you into high gear so you can shed unhealthy habits. The harder you work, the more you're driven to achieve your goals.

Shake Up Your Sex Life

Another place Mars likes to win is between the sheets. Venus may rule love, but Mars rules the sex drive, and views sex as fun and games. So, family and the responsibilities that come with having one aren't very appealing to this bed-hopping guy. The only time he gets obsessed is if the object of his desire slams the door in his face. Pluto craves a soul-shaking relationship based on his dark desire for absolute control. Don't think he's any sort of romantic, though. Obsession's the name of his game.

Sexual desires can erupt with renewed passion as Pluto's stalker-like need to bond merges with Mars's lusty appetite. Just make sure that you don't wake up in your next-door-neighbor's bed. This is one of the houses in which the itch to cheat can get out of control—especially if your primary relationship more closely resembles that of *Mad Men's* Don Draper instead of Brad and Angelina.

First-house energy is Masculine. The urge to prove yourself as sexy as ever can be tough on the object of your affection. Pluto kidnapped the object of his desire, Proserpina (Persephone), took her down to the underworld, and made her his queen. Like him, you may feel a surge of sexual energy and want to renew that gotta-have-you-now lust you felt when your relationship was new. But your partner might not appreciate your lurking in the dark then springing naked from behind the couch. However, this period of self-renewal can be full of erotic fun, especially if your relationship has settled into the once-a-week quickie. The caution is not to let sex become a battlefield, which can be a real threat, especially if uncomfortable issues arise from the past. The key is to rekindle the romance in little ways, and communicate your feelings to your partner in a nonthreatening manner.

Another expression of this potent energy is that you might unintentionally project *I'm available* signals. When your sexual confidence is high, other people's libidos perk up too. So don't be surprised if you're the target of random acts of flirting.

If you're single, this transit can bring a slew of possible partners. Sounds great, right? Well, there's a catch. Pluto tests are designed to make you look beneath the surface to the truth. Are you looking for a series of one-night stands? Are you searching for a long-term relationship? Are you using sex as a power game? You could also attract people who exhibit any of these traits.

Maybe you've been playing the field for a long time and you're tired. Pluto's reclusive energy might make you want to step away from the fray for a while. Do it. Shedding your old behaviors is part of the process. If you've made a series of mistakes and recognize there is a pattern, congratulate yourself. Refocus the Mars energy of this transit on other physical activities instead. Anything that challenges your stamina and makes you sweat will strengthen your body and help heal your heart.

Breaking the Pattern

Each Pluto transit pushes your soul to evolve. In the first house, it's about shedding the superficial behaviors that give a false impression of who you are. A first-house transit reinforces your separate identity and brings up self-image issues. If you work with this potent force, you'll build the confidence to recognize and rid yourself of the ingrained habits and self-perceptions you've been conditioned to believe since childhood. These defense mechanisms may have protected you or helped you survive so far, but Pluto's arrival signals that you don't need them anymore.

Here's a self-awareness exercise to try: When someone asks you how you are, instead of responding with the prepackaged "fine," take a couple of seconds to think before answering. Are you fine? Maybe you're having a wonderful day. Say so. Maybe you're frazzled because you have a dozen errands and not enough time. Say that. And you don't have to give a ten-minute download. The point is to make yourself stop and think about how you really feel, and then say it. In doing so, you start reversing those conditioned responses. Mindfulness, staying in the moment, focus—it's an old process, but it works.

Sure, all of this takes practice. And yes, you'll most likely encounter fallout from people who aren't used to hearing the truth, even a small truth. But don't let that stop you, and don't get discouraged. When you walk in awareness of what's going on in your life, you learn how to recognize the patterns that trigger your auto-responses. It takes time, but you have time. The reason Pluto's visits are decades long is to give you the chance to make permanent changes. To do that, you must admit your part in hiding behind the mask and risk the courage to take it off. When you do, you'll start living a more authentic life.

PLUTO IN THE SECOND HOUSE

The Phoenix of Values

At a Glance: The Second House

Imagine a bank vault. The second house contains our attitude toward money, possessions, and our personal value system. Are we penny-pinching or a sucker for a get-rich-quick scheme? Are we basically generous or greedy with our money, our time, and/or our affection? Security and safety are other important themes of the second house. Possessions, including people, are jealously guarded. This home corresponds to the toddler who screams, "Mine, mine, mine," when someone else picks up his toys.

The Money Wars

Your Quick Pick ticket just won ten thousand dollars. What do you do? Blow it on a weekend in Rio or pay the bills? Think carefully, because your choice can make or break you when Pluto's running the lotto.

The traditional definition of the second house is the House of Money and Values. Venus owns the place, and this chick is the original Material Girl. But security-loving Taurus the Bull lives here too. Blend these two, and the basic perspective on life becomes ownership. Possessions make Taurus feel safe. Pricey goods make Venus happy. Although money and what it buys is often the obsession, the fundamental principle of the second house is self-worth.

Born with Pluto in his second house, Len's war with money started early. His parents equated cash with security. Although they were financially stable, his parents used money as a method to control him. He rarely had extra to spend, and when he managed to beg a few dollars more on special occasions, he'd have to pay back the "loan." Threats of being cut out of the will were also standard. When Len found after-school work, his father discontinued his allowance, effectively voiding his chance to be self-sufficient. This type of dysfunctional attitude exhibited by a parental figure toward money is often present with a natal second-house Pluto.

When Len announced that he wanted to be an actor, his father used all of his intimidating arguments to frighten him into giving up. But this time, nothing worked, and Len left home. Fast-forward ten years. From the outside, Len lived a charmed life. Talented and driven, he'd fought his way to the head of Hollywood's A-list and had a hit TV show. He was also married to his gorgeous costar.

Although he'd had the courage to take a risk on himself, Len became obsessed with material possessions. He measured his personal value by what he could buy. Cash was his security, and the more he made, the more he spent. Len didn't value himself, so he tried to buy the love he'd never felt. Unfortunately, he ended up treating the people in his life like his possessions, too, including his wife.

At the height of Len's stardom, he made and lost several fortunes. Finally, after years of excess, his life crumbled. Pluto despises needless waste, so he yanked the chain on Len's finances, and the money swirled out of his life as quickly as it had arrived. His TV show was canceled, and his fans found another hero. The Lamborghini sitting in the driveway was repossessed. His marriage ended.

Behavior patterns such as Len's can be unconsciously aimed at the adults who abused the power of financial responsibility during that person's childhood. Failure as revenge is one of the darkest motivations of a second-house natal Pluto. Sure, Len's public ruin embarrassed his parents, but he destroyed his own career in the process.

Whether you're born with Pluto in the second house or he's paying yours a visit, you're not likely to earn, then lose, a fortune. However, the themes of money as power, self-worth, and/or taking a risk on yourself appear in each instance. *Mine* is the mindset of this home. *What can I buy, earn, collect, or (sometimes) steal to ensure I have security?* In this pad, Pluto becomes the banker who holds the keys to the safe containing whatever you value most. You're challenged to take an honest look at what's in your safe. Is it an accumulation of possessions at any cost? Emotional security at any price?

Perhaps you've fought your way up the corporate ladder or you're plugging away in your family business. You could be a self-made millionaire or need two jobs to make ends meet. Chances are that whatever you do for a living won't feel right once Pluto hits the front door. Many people with this placement or transit make dramatic life changes. In one drastic second-house transformation, Jeffery, an ER doctor, became a cowboy. He gave up his high-paying career to move across the country and become a team roper on the rodeo circuit. Yes, it sounds crazy, but his story is a perfect example of an extreme Plutonian act.

Of course, most people won't be as radical. However, Pluto's challenges deal with taking risks. Maybe you'll finally tell your domineering parent to get the hell off your back at the risk of being disowned. You might decide to go back to school in midlife and use part of your retirement fund to pay for it.

Winning the money wars requires taking responsibility for the way you've handled your material resources. As a mindfulness exercise, think about these questions: What childhood messages did you receive about money? How do you think that has affected your financial approach? Do you blow your paycheck and live on credit cards? Are you afraid to spend a nickel for fear of starving in your old age?

During this transit, it's time to consider whether you are still acting on or rebelling against the influence of those who had control of the money in your family.

Hand Up or Hand Out?

Another side of money management gone wrong is receiving the childhood message that someone else will always take care of you. You're either pampered, spoiled, and given everything your parents can afford to hand over, or your parents fail to teach you the basics of handling money. These scenarios are also based on control, usually by overprotective parents who have kind intentions. But the results can be just as disastrous.

Leanne never worried about money. When she was single, her parents bailed her out whenever she screwed up her budget. When she was married, her husband sweated over the budget while she racked up the bills. When they got divorced, she got the house and borrowed against her inheritance to pay him off. After her parents died, her financial counselor cut her a check every time she wanted to buy a new toy.

The message Leanne received had been that someone else would always provide for her. When she grew up and married, her husband would support her, just like her father had supported their family. But her life didn't work out that way, and after two divorces, she was alone, trying to make ends meet. When Pluto moved into her second house, she started to feel the pressure of her growing debt and shrinking bank account.

Instead of tightening her budget belt, she ignored the warning signs and spent as much as always. When her portfolio took a major hit during a stock-market crisis, she consulted her financial advisor. He told her she still had adequate funds *if* she carefully managed them in the future. Leanne's head was buried so deeply in the sands of denial that all she heard was *adequate*. At age sixty, she was still trying to make someone else take care of her.

Leanne continued to live on the financial edge, buying more clothes, taking trips, and driving a gas-guzzling car. Even when squeezed with costly repairs to her aging home, she refused to wise up. Instead, she jumped on the credit-card carousel and began juggling her debt from one interest-free offer to another.

Today, Pluto's about halfway through his visit to her second house. Has she learned her lesson? Nope. She's still scraping by and still refusing to change her lifestyle.

How many people do you know who are living beyond their means without a thought to the future? Are you one of them? Everyone makes mistakes and everyone does things they wish they hadn't, but when you systematically and continually turn your life over to others without taking responsibility, and then act as if the world owes you everything, you're not only being foolish, you're setting yourself up for a Pluto crash of galactic proportions.

That's what Pluto's here to remind you of, and he's not above taking everything you have to prove it. But don't panic. Most of Pluto's lessons don't include losing everything you own and moving to the backseat of your car. However, you are being asked to take a serious look at whether you control your finances or they control you.

Suffering financial hardship or ruin that you've brought on yourself isn't the only danger during this transit. You could run into swindlers and con artists of all types who are eager to separate you from your last dime. Today's world is full of scam scum, and everyone is a potential target. But you may have them crawling out of the proverbial woodwork while Pluto's in your second house. This is a good time to get a financial checkup, change the passwords to your online accounts and ATM card, and protect any other areas where your money is involved.

Cultivate Your Moral Resources

Another second-house theme that Pluto scrutinizes is your personal value system. What do you do to benefit others—do you write checks? Do you volunteer? Do you treat your friends and family fairly, or do you try to manipulate the outcome so that you get the largest share of everything, from the pizza to Grandma's collectibles?

If your values are tied to a rigid belief system that condemns or excludes everyone that isn't just like you, you're about to get a shock. *Profiling* is a term we've all heard many times. Usually, it's attached to racism, but everyone profiles everyone else in some way. What's your auto-response when you see a person who dresses differently than you? Maybe she's wearing an old sweatshirt and has unkempt hair. Perhaps she's in a designer outfit and stepping out of a Jaguar. What about the man with the southern drawl and rattling truck? Or the tattooed guy in line ahead of you at the bank?

Taurus, the sign that lives in the second house, is described as judgmental. As Fixed Earth, Taurus frequently believes it's always right. However, there are two sides to this coin. Whom do you judge, and who judged you? Were you told you'd never amount to anything? Were you expected to be the family success story? Did you hear that your class, race, sex, or religion was better than everyone else's? Can you see how that conditioning might affect you today?

Pluto's moral challenges are designed to make you open your eyes to ways in which you may devalue other people. He does this by ensuring that you come face to face with the folks you usually try to avoid. Maybe Mr. Tattoo turns out to be the head chef at your favorite pricey restaurant, or Ms. Bed Head is your grade schooler's favorite teacher.

When Pluto and Venus connect, obsessions flare. In the second house, greed can rear its ugly head—and so can self-denial. Either extreme causes the same outcome. Moral delinquency.

As another example, say that both Mr. A and Ms. B come from middle-income families who live in a neighborhood where everyone knows everyone's business, gossip, and bra size. Their respective parents stretch every dollar but they also manage to provide a few extras for their children, save a little for emergencies, and give some to charity. They aren't materially wealthy, but they are rich in ethical values and self-worth.

That's not good enough for Ms. B, though. She's craved things that are beyond her means from a very early age. She wishes she owned a house overlooking the Pacific and had a closetful of designer clothes. Although there is absolutely nothing wrong with wanting a better life than her parents, each time she watches Dad and Mom march off to work, she simultaneously feels guilt and shame for wishing that her parents were rich.

That's when the greed obsession takes over. She becomes a workaholic who never shares a penny with *anyone*. And she's a compulsive spender who accumulates objects that have no meaning to her, thinking that having these status symbols will make her feel secure and self-confident.

In the meantime, Mr. A views the same family scenario as a lesson in learning to live without. He grows up guilty and ashamed too, but sees himself as the eternal victim. He lives on a bare-bones budget and never shares a penny with anyone either. He's trying to find self-worth through self-denial.

One grasps for more and the other gives up everything, but neither finds the security they crave. Pluto dislikes a victim mentality as much as unbridled greed. Although the dysfunctional patterns are different, these two cases demonstrate the opposite sides of the self-appreciation coin. We can't expect others to fly to our rescue nor can we depend on the material world to remain constant. We must instead learn how to create our own inner security through independence. We also can't deny ourselves the pleasures of sharing our material and moral wealth with others, as we'll never spiritually evolve otherwise.

Fighting for Respect

A Pluto transit always churns up unresolved issues. Some of these are long-buried dreams that refuse to die. These nagging ideas that keep popping in your head are the universe's way of telling you that you're probably on the right path. Should you choose to walk it, prepare to meet at least one critic who'll try to shoot holes in your vision. In the second house, money as power is usually the roadblock.

From the outside, Kristen looked as if she had a wonderful life. She was a popular chef in a four-star restaurant and had a loving family and friends. Then Pluto arrived and ripped off her happy-face facade. Although she had intended to open her own restaurant before she was thirty, Kristen traded her dream—as many people do—for a steady paycheck. And whenever she'd bring up the subject, her husband would remind her of the many reasons why they couldn't afford to take the risk.

Then Kristen was handed the chance to have her restaurant, and that was when the real power struggle began. When she told her husband, he'd barely begun to recite his standard laundry list of reasons why it wasn't a good idea when she erupted in anger. Intentional or not, he'd been laying a guilt trip on her for years, and she'd kept going along for the ride. Her husband felt ambushed, and Kristen felt as if she were fighting for her life. Once the dust settled and Kristen's husband had picked his jaw up off of the floor, she laid out her plan. This time, she didn't ask or muse or discuss. She gave him facts, figures, and a timetable instead.

Of course, this only caused another argument. Kristen had to learn to assume her personal power without robbing her husband of his. And he had to realize that her desire to have her own business was not a threat to his abilities as a provider. They both needed to learn how to respect each other's contributions to their financial picture.

Eventually, they agreed on a plan that would allow her to go into business while reassuring him that they wouldn't go broke. Their compromise not only worked but Kristen's restaurant is flourishing.

During the years that Pluto moves through your second house, you can expect others to resist being pushed out of their comfort zones. He'll also push you out of yours by presenting opportunities to profit from both your talents as well as the challenges designed to test your value systems.

Body and Soul

The connection between Venus and Taurus is a sensual one—the physical senses of the second house are sensory. Sight, smell, taste, touch, and sound are all part of the natural experiences that bring us comfort and peace.

Our mind–body bond is inseparable. If we're sick or hungover or out of shape, we may feel depressed or guilty. If we're stressed or angry, our resistance is lower, and we may catch the latest flu bug.

Pluto's stroll through your second house brings up questions about how you're treating yourself. Are you stuck indoors at work all day and then sitting in front of the TV or glued to your laptop all night? Do you take time to appreciate the natural beauty in your life?

Even if you live in a high-rise apartment, you can look up at the sky or find a farm stand to walk through. Or drop by a florist shop and inhale the fragrance of fresh-cut flowers.

These are the years to start indulging yourself on a regular basis. Pamper yourself with whatever feels luxurious to you. Develop a creative talent. Get out of the house and enjoy nature. Walk more. Sit on a beach or have a backyard picnic. Turn off the TV and listen to music. Anything you do to awaken your senses to the physical joys of life is especially beneficial while Pluto travels through your second house.

Another side of bodily pleasure seeking is sex, and your sexuality could be an area that you need to review. Pluto rules physical desire. His home on the zodiac wheel is the eighth house, which is opposite the second. Sex in the eighth house is connected to long-term relationships and marriage. In the second house, the focus is on you and how you view your body as an object of desire.

As always, the childhood messages we received affect us as adults. Is sex sinful? Is it a duty? Repulsive? Boring? If any of these descriptions ring true for you, it's likely that you'll meet a hottie who can change your mind—*if* you're willing. Or your passion may reignite but in a deeper way, one that allows you to connect with your partner on a spiritual as well as a physical plane.

This transit is about taking quality time for yourself and learning to love your body, the home of your soul. By experiencing simple physical pleasures, your mind relaxes and your spirit grows. As you become mindful of how you mentally feel and how that affects your physical well-being, you can begin to clear away bad habits that eventually harm your health. One of Pluto's second-house tasks is to remind you that your body is your most precious possession. When you love it, it will love you.

Breaking the Pattern

Security without independence isn't worth the price. Pluto's objective in your second house is to teach you to steward both your financial and your moral resources. During these years, you're asked to examine your value systems and to take an honest look at the way you manage money.

You can learn how to free yourself from family prejudices and unreal financial expectations. When money issues arise, learn to compromise. One way is to ask yourself *Is this something I truly need?* before succumbing to an impulse buy.

Nurture your body, inside and out. Indulging physical pleasures and tending your physical body are part of this journey. How you care for yourself during these years can affect you for the rest of your life.

Be mindful of how you treat people who are different than you too. Preconceived judgments about others are usually false. Treating people as individuals instead of lumping them into categories helps to erase the fear or prejudice you may have learned as a kid.

Working through the issues Pluto reveals takes time and effort, but the process is slow and steady, allowing you to make adjustments that set you on the path to understanding that the only true security lies within you.

PLUTO IN THE THIRD HOUSE

The Phoenix of Truth

At a Glance: The Third House

Think of a newsroom. In the third house, the soul begins to communicate with others by gathering, processing, and disbursing information of all sorts. Truth, rumor, and gossip live here. So do cell phones, social networks, and the let's-do-lunch bunch—all babbling 24/7. Do we tell the truth? Stretch it? Ignore or hide it? Third house watchwords are *text, talk,* and *tell anyone who'll listen,* but are we really communicating?

Talk, Talk, Talk

When Pluto moves into your third house, life can begin to resemble a courtroom drama. Mercury, the planet of communication in all its forms, rules this place. Mutable-Air Gemini lives here, as do your siblings, neighbors, and the people you see every day. Gemini is social and curious, but in a superficial way (soul-searching conversations make the Twins uncomfortable).

Mercury is a storyteller. He can talk the spots off a leopard and twist facts into all kinds of entertaining tales. The pure Mercurial nature is a conduit of information. He gathers the latest info, adds his angle on the story, then blabs to anyone within earshot, but he skims the details and glosses over the facts in a rush of topical conversation.

Pluto is the king of brutal honesty. Although he's tight-lipped and secretive about his world, when he does speak, he demands truth. Think of an uncompromising investigative journalist who won't stop probing until she uncovers all the facts. Pluto's energy penetrates beneath the surface. And when Pluto travels into Mercury's territory, the conversation gets intense.

These two know each other well. Mercury was Jupiter's youngest son and Pluto's nephew. His reputation as a silver-tongued negotiator is legendary. When Pluto tricked Ceres's (Demeter's) daughter Proserpina (Persephone) into becoming his queen in Hades, Jupiter chose to send Mercury to bargain for Proserpina's freedom. Although the negotiations were somewhat successful, Mercury's slick arguments couldn't dazzle Pluto, he only agreed to allow Proserpina to spend six months of each year above ground.

Third-house communication between Mercury and Gemini is detached. Ask a question, get an answer, don't probe the undercurrents. Imagine a cocktail party where the guests circulate through the room blowing air kisses and exchanging glib conversation. Everyone's having a great time because no one's talking about anything controversial. Suppose Frank has a couple of drinks and starts barbing his friend Dan. Dan brushes off Frank's rudeness with humor or rationalization, or some other excuse. But Frank's overworked. He's drunk. Dan doesn't want to spoil the party with a confrontation.

Now, think of the same cocktail party, same scene—only, Pluto's milling through the crowd. Frank confronts Dan, but this time, he gets right to the point and accuses Dan of flirting with his wife. Dan gets angry and defensive. Tempers flare. They may shout or shove or even punch each other. How does that make everyone feel—uncomfortable? Embarrassed? A variety of reactions will ripple through the room. This is Pluto's goal. He wants the truth, and he's willing to cause a nasty scene to get it.

The third house process of trying to intellectualize the truth seems like a good idea—*Let's be rational.* However, what usually happens is that we only skim the surface without solving anything. That's why third-house communications can sound like broken records. The discussions are endless, but the problems are never resolved because we've buried the truth, and we sure don't want to face how we feel about it. Transiting Pluto brings up situations you've lived with for years that now reach the boiling point, forcing you to deal with them.

Word Power

A sibling puts you down then pleads, "Just kidding." You're told that Uncle Joe is on a business trip when you've overheard your sobbing aunt describe his jail cell. Your parent says something hurtful that's "for your own good."

Maybe *you're* the one with a tongue that could cut stone. Most of us have been the target of verbal barbs or abuse, and most of us have said mean things.

When Pluto appears in the third house, either by birth or through a transit, we're asked to confront the deeper meanings behind the way we've been taught to think about ourselves and the world around us. *Children should be seen and not heard. Just ignore your brother's teasing. Mom doesn't mean it when she yells.* Pluto peels away the insulating layers of excuses that protect us from the sometimes bitter truth.

From the outside, Elaine's childhood home looked like a scene from *The Cosby Show*. Inside, it was pure Tennessee Williams. As a child, Elaine coped by filling journals with the emotions she wasn't allowed to show. Later, she developed a caustic sense of humor that was both a way to express her feelings and to avoid real intimacy.

As an adult, Elaine suffered through a series of verbally abusive relationships, sometimes as the victim but more often the perpetrator. Worse, she perpetuated the third-house cover-up she'd learned from her parents by pretending that everything was fine. After a particularly gruesome argument with her third husband, Elaine had a flashback to a similar fight she'd witnessed between her parents, and that was the breakthrough that allowed her to see her own truth. Words were the weapons she'd always used to protect herself by verbally shooting first before the other person could wound her.

Third-house energy is expressed in a variety of ways. Some clients state that they have always been hesitant to speak up, for fear of creating problems in their relationships. Others take the offense-is-the-best-defense road and act like a prosecuting attorney hammering away at a hostile witness. Or they swing between the two as Elaine did. Some third-house Pluto souls say they write better than they speak, while others communicate through art, photography, or music.

Think about how you communicate. Are you skeptical of what people say to you, especially compliments? *What did he mean by that? What does she want from me?* The difference between evolving beyond the superficiality of the third house and revolving through Pluto's shadow side of coercion is to consider not just what you hear but how you interpret it. Why are you suspicious of a friendly word? Why do you brush aside a compliment? Could it be because, deep down, you don't think anyone could possibly have anything good to say to or about you? Conversely, what messages are you sending when you speak? Think about not only what you say but how you say it.

Authority Issues

Natal Pluto bestows a naturally suspicious nature. If you were born with this placement, you were most likely the family truth-teller—or tried to be, because you came into the world with a built-in BS detector. You're a deep thinker and are instinctively right most of the time. You can sift the nuggets of truth from a bushel of fiction.

As a kid, you zeroed in on what was unsaid and innocently asked questions. When you did, you were either told to shut up or sent to your room for being nosy. And even though you may have been thumped for your trouble, this only fueled your curiosity.

You could sense a lie before you knew what that word meant—because your impressions came directly from Pluto's crystal-clear eyes. Your instincts were fine-tuned and usually right on target. The problem was that the adults made the rules. They created a reality they could live with and tried to force it on you, as your insight threatened to shatter the family fantasy.

The third house is stuffed with propaganda. For better or worse, the influences you received—from a look or a careless word or an overheard conversation—became the voice in your head that still tells you how to handle everyday life. You knew you weren't hearing the truth, but you didn't have the power to stand up to the authority figures glossing the facts. So you grew up suspicious of anyone who tried to tell you what to do, or you acted as if he or she had all the answers. You may still be operating under the family gag order. Or are you so outspoken that you alienate others? Either extreme isn't healthy.

The strength of this placement is that you are a natural teacher in the classic sense. You can help others think for themselves and find their true voice. You can also become the voice of the powerless. Dr. Martin Luther King, Jr. was born with Pluto in the third house. Think of how eloquent and direct his words were. Although verbally abused and threatened, he wasn't intimidated. He never stopped speaking the truth about an issue that had been suppressed and largely ignored by an entire country.

Trust is always a Pluto issue. In the third house, it's about sharing your deepest feelings through conversation. Revealing a small confidence helps you to get started. Then the other person shares one of hers, and the bond strengthens. Little by little, you learn how to speak your truth without fear of being shushed up or put down.

Tell It Like It Is

Pluto's presence always signals an awakening to the contradictions between your social conditioning and the truth. When Pluto transits your third house, you should brace for a trip to the dead-letter office in your mind. He storms in and the locks melt and the rusty hinges swing open, exposing the lies you've learned to live with. If you're used to rationalizing your past or have buried it so deeply that you don't recognize what really happened, get ready to enter the Halls of Truth.

During this transit, you'll find that you are no longer willing to settle for simplistic explanations or rationalization. Many times, we aren't even aware that we're operating on a superficial level—not until Pluto brings up a problem that we've shoved to the back of our mind through the years.

This cycle is about diving into the deepest part of your mind and confronting any demons still living there. As with every Pluto transit, the repetitive patterns that keep you hooked in dysfunction will rear their nasty heads again. In the third house, all are connected through the written or spoken word.

Pluto operates in the shadows. If you don't deal with the shadow side of yourself or your life, he'll show it to you through the people you know. An old family conflict could flare. You might meet a person who triggers a gut-level response that makes you uncomfortable. Whatever the catalyst, mindless excuses won't work. Neither will those repetitive vent sessions that exhaust you because you never take action. Although talking is a natural Mercury function, when Pluto joins the conversation, past angers, jealousies, and resentments flare. Though you may have talked about and around these issues until you're blue, you still haven't resolved anything.

Perhaps you don't feel like talking or it's no longer as easy to have casual conversations. You may become more cynical, suspecting deception and whitewashing by everyone in your life—especially those who hold the power. Paranoia is also a Pluto trait. His trek through your head can feel as if you're caught in a complex thriller plot where the truth's been massaged so much that you can't believe anything. Don't panic. All of this is designed to help you rid yourself of the unresolved conflicts of the past. When you do decide to talk, just be honest.

During Pluto's transit, you're in a long period of separating what you instinctively know to be true from what you were told to believe. Just because *it's always been that way*, doesn't mean it's right. Pluto questions everything. So should you. If you do, he will supply the courage you need to confront these issues and free your voice. Yes, it's tough. However, the more honest you are with yourself and others, the easier this transit will be.

Every Pluto transit brings a feeling of loss. Pluto's power of destruction is also the key to transformation—the symbol of extreme events that change our lives. The death associated with Pluto is rarely about physical death. It's a sense of losing some part of you. Do you feel like you've never been listened to? Or do you feel guilty because of something you did or didn't say in the past? If you've been afraid to speak out, this transit makes you realize that it's time to say exactly what you mean.

The trick is in learning how to be truthful without alienating the people you want to keep in your life. Although Pluto is as frank as a fist in the face, you won't get away with being as brutally honest. The third house encourages two-way communication, and you have to be able to take what you dish out. While you must state your opinion, don't unleash your rage or sarcasm on the other person. That said, if you finally get the guts to tell someone who's harmed you to go to hell, that's okay too. Just be sure that you know the difference.

Family Plots and Sibling Rivalry

When Pluto hangs his coat on your family tree, prepare to relive all sorts of unfinished or unhealthy business. This could be anything from a direct attack on you by a brother or a sister to your helping him or her live a different lifestyle than your family intended.

During Pluto's tour of your third house, emotions that have simmered in your gut for years could erupt. Sure, you can handle it with another angry outburst, but that will get you nowhere—it hasn't so far. Wait out the urge to yell and throw the dishes. Think. Are you reliving something from the past that can't be changed? Replaying a broken record of blame? When you're out to break heads instead of breaking through the lies you've lived with, you're operating from the same negative energy as those who may have hurt you. Becoming your mean sister or meddling uncle won't solve anything.

In the third house, Pluto tries to expose whatever you've either deliberately ignored or subconsciously suppressed for the wrong reasons. Pluto is introspective—he operates underground and away from people. During this transit, you're challenged to travel inside your memory and think about the difference between your perception of the messages you received in childhood and what you were really told to believe. Pluto acts like the deprogrammer who reverses the brainwashing you've been fed. Maybe you were told you weren't as smart as your siblings. Perhaps you were taught to smile no matter what—*Don't make waves*, or *Don't question authority*. All of these messages have been influencing you since the moment you first heard them.

Now is the time to examine your self-perception. When faced with a new opportunity, what's your gut-level reaction? *I could never accomplish that, so why try? If I did succeed, I'd probably get hit by a bus the day after I hit it big.* Did someone tell you that you couldn't succeed or shouldn't try? Did your parents feel that way about their lives? Try to remember the stories behind such negative feelings and where you received those messages. You may have to go through a period of self-examination that stirs up painful memories before you uncover the real story. Don't give up, and don't be afraid. The only way to break down the wall of misconception is to knock it down.

The youngest of three brothers, Anton spent most of his childhood in and out of bed with various undiagnosed illnesses. Conversely, his oldest brother, Bryce, was a high school football hero who won an athletic scholarship to college, and his middle brother, Jason, was handsome and outgoing.

One of Anton's first conscious memories was that of his Aunt Ellen telling him not to bother about being the runt of the family. "Even if you were normal, you couldn't keep up with either of your brothers," she'd said. When he told his mother, she told him not to pay attention to his aunt's remarks because, "That's just the way she talks." So he learned two things very early. He wasn't normal because he was small and frail, and other people were allowed to talk to him any way they chose and he had to ignore the hurtful remarks.

From his perspective, unless he was sick, he was largely disregarded. As adults, Bryce became an investment counselor, Jason sold insurance, and Anton earned a PhD in psychology and opened his own practice. However, anytime the three were together, Anton was still treated like the sickly little brother the other two felt free to pick on or ignore.

Although, as a therapist, Anton helped others to uncover suppressed memories and find their voices, he still couldn't speak up for himself. When issues arose at work or in his marriage or with his children, he either sidestepped the problem, tried to rationalize it, or got a bellyache.

Enter Pluto. Anton's old hurts, jealousies, and competition for parental love and approval reared their ugly heads. At first, he tried his usual avoidance mechanisms, but nothing worked. One day, he decided to call Bryce and honestly open up for the first time. What he received in return was Bryce's anger for the way their mother had always "coddled" Anton. Bryce felt that Anton had faked his illnesses to get attention. Anton was shocked because he'd always felt like the victim. And Bryce had suffered because of his own guilt about not being able to live up to the football-hero message he'd received; he never felt successful enough.

Both brothers had been handed a false value system by which to measure their self-worth. After a tense couple of hours on the phone, they had cleared the air enough to agree to talk more. Anton suggested they include Jason, and Bryce concurred. If they had been caught in the family propaganda, he probably had too.

When long-buried resentments begin to seethe in you or a sibling and finally erupt, the result could cause a permanent break in your relationship. If you find yourself facing this kind of showdown, stop to think before you shout. Flipping into screaming-little-kid mode will only have you and your sister repeating a childhood fight, or you and your brother punching and kicking as you roll around the lawn again.

To save the relationship, you'll need to act like an adult as Anton did. Use the power of Pluto to resist repeating a tired scenario and try to get to the truth. Did your sibling feel you were your parents' favorite kid? Did you feel that way about him or her? This is your chance to clear up misunderstandings, resolve issues, and build a healthier relationship as the three brothers have.

When Pluto moves through your third house, you could also become closer to a sibling who's always been secretive or distant. You may discover that you can help your parents understand why your brother is in self-destruct mode or your sister just eloped with an unemployed circus clown half her age.

On the other hand, if you've suffered mental or physical abuse from a sibling, this powerful energy can give you the courage and the voice to cut the ties that bind, telling him or her to get permanently lost. Pluto says that even some relatives don't deserve to know you.

When Pluto comes to dinner, the food fights resume. Whether they're as innocent as a forkful of mashed potatoes or as hazardous as a skillet full of sizzling oil, you can take control of the situation. Pluto awakens the power within you to either reconcile or refuse to be the victim ever again.

Breaking the Pattern

Even before we learn to speak, we absorb the power of words—their ability to wound and to evade. As with every Pluto transit, he doesn't care whether you clean house or get kicked out of the house. His purpose is to rattle the bars so loudly that you acknowledge you're locked in an emotional jail. Even though someone else might have built it, the truth is that you've chosen to keep living there. You're your own jailer, and you've held the key in your hand all along. Your challenge is to unlock the door and set yourself free.

If you learn to listen to yourself, you can break those destructive patterns and reframe them into healthier behaviors. During this transit, your words will carry more emotional weight, whether you want them to or not. Consider how you can frame what you want to say in an honest, charitable way—without vengeance. You do this by learning to temper Pluto's cut-to-the-chase directness with Mercury's verbal shadow boxing.

Get to the point. Make sure the other person understands exactly what you mean, but state your case in the calmest possible manner. Debunking the family myth or busting a shiny bubble of fantasy is healthy. Speak with dignity, not destructiveness. The people you confront might not agree with or accept what you say, but that's their choice. This isn't about them. It's about you.

Once you begin to think for yourself, question the status quo, and say what's really on your mind, you'll grow stronger. Each time you speak the truth, you'll gain more courage to stand up to the people who've held you back. You'll stop walking around with word packages falling out of your mouth and find your true voice.

PLUTO IN THE FOURTH HOUSE

The Phoenix of Nurturing

At a Glance: The Fourth House

Home sweet home of the past, present, and future resides in the fourth house. This place represents our parents, family members, and how well we nurture others and ourselves. Our perception of home and family and what those terms mean are developed here. Are we bound by tradition or is home anywhere we drop our socks? Is it a haven to run to or a place we'd like to run from?

The fourth house also represents the literal space in which we live. In the fourth house, the soul is beginning to learn how to connect with others through shared space and family ties.

Home or Haunted House?

It's midnight. The doors are locked, the shades are drawn, and you're home alone in the dark. Pluto is the bogeyman who throws the closet open and lets the monsters out.

Infants feel emotion long before they learn language, and emotions are powerful communication systems. These earliest patterns define whether we're imprinted with a sense of love and nurturing, neglect, or unpredictable attention. The people you call family live here, but during Pluto's visit, this place can be anything but home sweet home. The folks in this pad include your ancestors, your childhood and present-day families, and your assorted relatives. Family history, tradition, and the ghosts of secrets past are contained in this space.

The fourth house is submerged in the watery depths of Cancer. This moody sign can swing from the mother of dysfunction to the essence of support and caring—all within about twenty minutes.

The ever-changing Moon rules this home. Moonlight distorts reality. It can mask the look of a dilapidated building or make a patch of nettles look soft and inviting. When Pluto sets up his flood-lights on the lawn, he forces you to see the peeling paint and dead grass. Pluto likes to snoop around the fourth house because the place is full of long-buried family dramas. Think of an old trunk covered in dust and hidden under a blanket in the corner of the attic. It's locked, and no one admits to knowing what happened to the key. No problem. Pluto's skeleton key fits, and he'll toss it to you. If you decide to open that rusty lock and start poking around, what you discover can either reinforce what you've always suspected or may send you reeling in shock.

Being born with Pluto in the fourth house or having this transit at an early age can be harsh. Your home life could have been over-shadowed with a sense of loss, or punctuated with uncomfortable silences or frightening arguments. Sometimes the loss of a parent comes through divorce or, more tragically, through death.

Maybe it's an alarming discovery about your birth as it was for Laura, who was twelve when she found her birth certificate while nosing through her mother's dresser. She discovered that her bio-logical father wasn't the man who had raised her. Sometimes the undercurrents of infidelity or substance abuse are involved, and one parent tries to protect you by making excuses for the offender.

Whatever the reason, your sense of security and faith in those you depended on were shaken at an early age and have periodically resurfaced in problematic ways. You may feel that you've never had control over your life. When relationships get tough, do you have a pattern of dumping first before you get dumped? Have you put your lovers or your spouse in the position of being your father or mother figure? Do you nurture everyone else without nurturing yourself? Maybe you had to take on some adult responsibilities when you were very young.

Swinging From the Family Tree

There are *all* kinds of trees (and nuts!) in the forest of family. You might come from a long line of bluebloods or a short line of con artists. You may be one of a horde of relatives or an only child. Maybe you were adopted or raised in foster homes, or you left home at an early age. No matter how you arrived or to whom, you have intense feelings about family. As a child, you were dependent on them, whether they were crazy or not. Your sense of what home means came from them. But as soon as Pluto steps onto the porch, the foundation begins to crack.

Pluto may rip the blinders off an unhappy childhood, forcing you to re-examine that phony, happy-family facade. Maybe the darkest surprise you uncover is that your great-great-grandfather was a bank robber.

Discovering family stories and secrets can arm you with the information to help solve a chain of mysteries that no one's been willing to discuss—especially your mother. These undercurrents often create a sense of anxiety that you can't name but you know exists, even if the adults pretend everything is peachy. You might discover that Mom was pregnant with you when she married Dad and wonder if you're the reason their marriage isn't happy. Should you feel guilty? Hell no! That's their issue. But knowing that doesn't help much if you feel unwanted or in the way.

Exposing this information, even if it's painful—and even if your parents refuse to discuss it—helps to ensure that the past doesn't determine your future. Asking your mom to spill the family beans is never easy. More than that, she and your father are dealing with the messages they received from their parents. Family chains of evasiveness are as hereditary as being born with your grandmother's red hair or your dad's dimpled chin. And reflecting on this might allow you to better understand their actions.

Pluto's presence, either by birth or transit, signals that something in the emotional foundation of your home needs fixing. A parent's avoidance of the truth can make your imagination work overtime.

Children assume that whatever's wrong is their fault, and you may carry a sense of shame or guilt into adulthood. Even if you have a solid marriage, happy kids, and a tight network of extended family, at your core, you may still feel alone and unworthy of love.

Think about how you see yourself within your family group. Do you feel like an outsider or as if you don't deserve the happiness you've found? Often, Pluto gives us a sense of impending doom wherever he lands, and we walk around waiting for disaster to strike. We're afraid of being too happy because we might suddenly lose everything.

You might not be able to get answers to your childhood family riddles, but you can begin to share your fears and frustrations with someone you trust today. Building a sense of security within yourself starts with forming a "family" you feel safe with. These are people with whom you feel a deep connection—kindred spirits. Sisters or brothers of your heart and soul. Lovers and partners who nurture you. Any way you build this clan is good. Tradition, marriage, blood ties, children—none are required. The point is to learn that the concept of home lies within you. And you have the power to build a safe environment no matter what your childhood home may have lacked.

Even if you feel that your family's virtues outweigh the flaws you discover, you're still likely to experience a surprise or two when Pluto's transit hits. One way he accomplishes this is by bringing people into your life who haven't been raised in such a healthy atmosphere. In these cases, you might be able to help them break free from a bad situation by becoming the person they can talk to without reservation.

More important, you could recognize an emotional hot spot you've unconsciously ignored about your "perfect" family. Maybe your parents tried to protect you from a hurtful truth or you blocked an uncomfortable one. One way or another, Pluto reveals some uneasy surprises that surround the concept of home.

Remember the fairy tale *The Three Little Pigs*? They hid in their straw, stick, and brick houses when the Big Bad Wolf came tramping through the neighborhood. In the story, the brick house kept the wolf at bay. Nothing can withstand Big Bad Pluto.

Sophia, who had been adopted into a large, loving family as an infant, never had the desire to search for her birth parents—not until Pluto jolted her sense of family at age thirty-five, when he moved into her fourth house. Pluto had reawakened the questions Sophia had thought about over the years. *Who am I?* she asked herself. *Why was I given away?* These and dozens of other questions flooded her head, and she started looking for her biological family. But she didn't have to wait long. Within a few weeks, she discovered that her birth mother and her half-sister were living in a neighboring town less than thirty miles away.

Although Sophia was eager to meet them, her adoptive mom became defensive. Sophia persisted and initiated contact anyway, but her birth mother refused to see her because her family knew nothing about Sophia. She'd been an unmarried teen who had tried to put the past behind her and build a new life. Thanks to Pluto's obsessive force, Sophia didn't give up, and eventually, her biological mother agreed to meet her. Sophia also met her half-sister. Sadly, neither relationship developed further than polite conversation.

After a period of alternating between anger and grief, Sophia realized that her perception of home and family didn't depend on either her birth parents or her adoptive parents. She had built a stable life with her husband and children, and was her own person. She had all the home she needed already.

David was also adopted into a loving family. And when he was diagnosed with a complicated learning disability, his parents were determined to find the best treatment possible. They chose a highly respected school, but because they lived far from the facility, David was enrolled as a boarded student. His family kept in constant contact and visited frequently, and David excelled. After a year, he was able to return home and attend public school with the help of a tutor.

Then David began to self-destruct. He was constantly in and out of trouble, and by his early teens, he started using drugs. His fourth-house Pluto had deepened David's fear of abandonment.

His unconscious mind assumed his adoptive family was rejecting him just as his birth parents had. However, in trying to punish them by acting out, he nearly killed himself. It took family therapy and the strong, unconditional love of his parents before David finally grew beyond his self-inflicted wounds.

Your family wounds may or may not be as deep as David's, or have the same outcome as Sophia's. However, when Pluto shuffles through your fourth house in his steel-toed slippers, he kicks up all kinds of drama. Your spouse acts like an uncaring heel. Your kids compete to see who can get to rehab the quickest. Uncle Sponge-Off-You-Bob asks to live in your spare bedroom. Sure, these messes happen to everyone. However, fourth-house family crises force you to examine your own role in either causing or covering up the carnage.

Another theme concerns your current family. You may begin to question your ability as a parent and a partner. You might see your children and spouse as a bunch of life-sucking vampires and decide to go on strike, refusing to cater to their demands. If you're having these types of feelings, it's time to regroup. Play victim with Pluto and he'll hold a mirror to your face. Collapse in a crying jag, blaming your selfish family for taking advantage of you, and he'll dredge up a childhood memory that makes you squirm. He'll show you how your actions are aiding and abetting your family's bad behaviors.

Did you self-sacrifice to keep the peace with your parents? Did you let your siblings push you around until you fell into a screaming fit of frustration? Blow your nose and take a hard look at how you respond to the challenges and responsibilities of family life. If your caregiving is out of control, you aren't helping your family. You're teaching them to be selfish. You aren't helping yourself either. Instead, you're building rage that will eventually destroy your home.

Try to be aware of how you react to the repetitive patterns of your family life. Do you ask for help when you need it? Do you automatically shrug your shoulders or roll your eyes in that here-we-go-again fashion before listening to what your kid or spouse is trying to tell you? A short, nonreactive pause to think before you speak can break an autopilot response.

Take a Break

Because Pluto is a recluse who loves his solitude, you might feel like staying home more often. If you've been at everyone else's beck and call, this is a good idea. Just make sure you don't go to bed and pull the covers over your head.

You could decide to shut out your childhood family's drama and focus on building a stronger relationship with your partner and/ or children. This is the time to examine your insecurities, discover your nurturing side, and use it to nurture yourself as well as others. It's important that you be good to yourself during a fourth-house transit. Get extra rest. Buy yourself a gift now and then. Engage in activities that make you happy.

Pluto won't allow you to play the blame game that transfers all responsibility to either your long-dead relatives or your living family members. He doesn't give a damn whether you live with the Waltons or the Borgias—this is your gig. It's *your* job to take charge, become your own enforcer, and make the changes that help you break away from the chokehold of the skeletons in your family closet.

Pluto challenges you to prove to yourself that you're much stronger than you believe. Feel like you've turned into a black sheep? Good. This transit is all about exposing the rules and double standards you were forced to accept. Once you let this hissing cat out of the bag, expect a variety of shocked and appalled reactions. Your parents might freak. Your sister might call you a nutcase. Aunt Matilda could threaten to never speak to you again, but that's okay. One less funeral for you to attend.

Maybe you become obsessed with curiosity about your family tree and make some shocking discoveries. So what? Just because you had a few jailbirds in your lineage doesn't mean that you're destined to be one. Embrace the information that opens your mind and acknowledge the truth, good or bad. You can't change the past, but you can evolve beyond it.

Pluto's mission is to help you survive no matter what that truth might be. Your mission is to make peace with the past and to learn that you have a choice. You don't have to be tied to people who cause you emotional or physical harm or stay in a situation that doesn't nurture and safeguard you. Pluto's tour of your fourth house will give you the courage to change the emotional landscape of the place you call home.

Home Sweet Home

The physical place you call home is also represented in the fourth house. During these years, you might decide to move to a new neighborhood, town, or country. You might also decide to renovate or discover that your home needs repair work. Pluto deals in buried problems. He peels the paint off the house to reveal the dry rot. But before you begin any major remodeling project, it's wise to look behind the scenes—during a fourth-house Pluto transit, it can be critical. Check the plumbing, foundation, and anything else that's hidden in the walls, under the house, or in the attic. Although Uranus rules the electrical system, Pluto controls the transfer of power from one area to another, so check the wiring too.

This is a good transit to slowly make changes that will add value to your home. Pluto's aim is to gain everything he can, including money. You might be interested in investing in real estate, but again, get the facts to make sure you know what you're doing. Mr. P doesn't suffer fools lightly—you could lose everything. You may also experience a sense of longing for a favorite home from your past.

Judy's Pluto transit led her to a bank-owned house in dire need of repair. The old two-story place reminded her of her grandparents' home, bringing back wonderful memories of her grandmother's dinners and her grandfather's garden of tomatoes, pole beans, and squash.

Although the house was in a beautiful, renovated neighborhood, Judy was concerned about the years it had stood vacant. It had housed drug dealers and at least one meth lab. She wanted the house but also wanted to rid it of that terrible energy. Because the price was so low, she made the choice to buy the property, tear it down, and rebuild a modern version of her grandparents' home.

This is what Pluto's energy is all about. You can peel away the darkness and negativity, and remake both your physical and emotional home—fresh, solid, and safe. Pluto isn't concerned with what you do, that's your decision. He just pitches the ball. It's up to you to hit it out of the park.

Breaking the Pattern

When Pluto occupies your fourth house, he brings opportunities to test what works and what doesn't with family members, your marriage, and your connection to your heritage. This transit isn't about shutting off contact, although you might feel the need to do that too. If so, that's okay. It's all in a day's work for Pluto. Pluto came here to shed light on family secrets, help you enlighten your family, and liberate you from the brainwashing that's held you down.

Start at the often-dreaded regular family gatherings, holiday celebrations, or reunions. Do you ever wonder why we commonly consider these get-togethers more duty than pleasure? Do you think it might be because people tend to unconsciously revert to their childhood roles the moment they step into the room?

Next time you attend one of these functions, observe the behaviors going on around you. Who's still acting like the family bully? Who's still demanding attention? Who's being patronizing? Is your dad trying to tell your forty-year-old brother how to slice the prime rib? Are you reverting to how you acted when you were a kid? Being conscious takes practice, but once you are, you can reverse your knee-jerk reactions.

Remaining loyal to family members is not the same as remaining stuck. You can love and respect a kind but misguided family. You can also forgive and move on from a dysfunctional one. Either way, you are not bound to carry on their traditions, nor are you predestined to wear their success or failure. When you acknowledge this, you begin freeing yourself to leave the patterns of your childhood home behind.

Pluto forces situations that are intended to bring change. It's important that you be good to yourself during this transit, because it's brimming with emotional excess. As difficult as it might be, disentangling yourself from family tradition and trauma is the only thing that will allow you to build a healthy family relationship in the future.

Pluto's visit to your fourth house is about discovering your ideal home and having the courage to create it your way, with whomever you choose. When you do, you'll understand how to care for every person you meet as well as the ones you consider your family. Best of all, you'll learn how to nurture yourself.

PLUTO IN THE FIFTH HOUSE

The Phoenix of Creativity

At a Glance: The Fifth House

Call this pad the playhouse. The fifth house just wants us to have fun. Our creative urges—including the desire to have children—live here. Kids, dogs, and circus performers run through the yard. Monkeys swing in the trees. Anything that can be remotely described as recreation (casual sex, compulsive gambling . . .) is piled high in this pleasure palace. The fifth house represents the part of our ego that wants to stand out from the crowd.

Raise the Curtain

The fifth house is called the House of Creativity, Children, and Romance. Although the children you have and the children you're close to are some of the themes of this area, the focus is on your inner child.

This is the zodiac's theater of self-expression, and a wall-to-wall mixed bag of discipline and hedonism. Romantics, kids, creative geniuses, and risk takers live here—and so do con artists and slackers. The Sun is the producer, drama-loving Leo is standing center stage, and the place is as full of critics as any playhouse on Broadway.

Both hubris and humility share space in this abode. As critic, Pluto will knock the phony modesty out of someone's hypocritical mouth. As backer, he'll bolster a fragile ego. Although Pluto can pop an overblown personality, most people don't have that issue. Remember the Cowardly Lion? During a fifth-house transit, you're asked to overcome the frightened part of yourself that worries *I'm not good enough*. If you aren't living up to your potential, it's time to think about who stifled your ego.

Allan and Jamal were lifelong friends and musicians who had a two-man band. Jamal sang, and Allan did everything else. He wrote the music, played guitar and keyboard, booked the gigs, staged the lighting, and even drove most of the time when they were on tour. Although Allan was the force behind their success, Jamal played the part of the star. He ignored their expense budget, managed to find something else to do when Allan was setting up the equipment, and shrugged his indifference as to where or when their next gig happened. Enter Pluto.

Allan and Jamal had driven more than fifteen hours straight to Portland from L.A. for a three-night show. After the last set, they were relaxing in the hotel bar when Allan snapped. What pushed him over the edge? Jamal had ordered a shot of ultra-expensive Laphroaig whiskey. Jamal's behavior hadn't changed. It was Allan's tolerance that had come to a screeching halt. The bar bill blew the lid off his internal pressure cooker, but Pluto had cranked the heat. As Allan put it, "We yelled all the way back to L.A."

Pluto had shattered the illusion, and Allan finally saw the truth— he was the talent that the crowd came to see. But he put up with Jamal's overblown ego because he thought he couldn't make it on his own. Because they were long-term buddies, whenever Allan's resentment bubbled up, he suppressed it to avoid causing problems. When Pluto moved into his fifth house, however, the lid blew. Although they managed to remain friends, Allan and Jamal never worked together again.

After the breakup, Allan got out of the music business altogether. And with the hustle of road trips and one-night stands over, he returned to his first creative passion—writing. Today, he's a successful author of paranormal thrillers.

Are you submerging your nature to keep the peace like Allan did? Are you afraid of stepping out of your (dis)comfort zone? What would make you happier—pursuing a creative passion? Having more leisure time? Getting out of the mainstream? Everyone has a secret dream that periodically nags them. Whatever yours is, the nag can become obsessive when Pluto's at the helm. Listen to it.

Pluto's arrival in your fifth house, by either transit or birth, signals a need to express your individuality. You are being asked to overcome your insecurity, so forget what others may think. Just create something that gives you joy. On a soul level, Pluto can help you become a pathfinder for others who need help bolstering their egos. Although this could mean a public life in the spotlight, it's more about healing your hurt inner child—about reclaiming the spontaneity and delight in life that's buried within you.

Step Backstage

Memories of those who laid down the rules that muffled your individuality will resurface during this transit. Maybe Father Killjoy called you a scatterbrain who'd never amount to anything. What about Auntie Proper Panties who cringed at the sight of your purple-streaked teenage hair? As a small child, you might have been taught that "showing off" was bad. But how can you find your path if you don't give a free rein to creative thinking? What's wrong with wanting recognition and approval?

As an adult, you carry the memory of the restraints that prevented you from ever fully enjoying life. And recovering that uninhibited spirit requires stepping into the past to examine the people who criticized you. What would you say instead to the little girl or boy you were? Say it to yourself now and make it your mantra. It's great to laugh and be silly. It's wonderful to dream big and want to be noticed. Pluto wouldn't be here if someone hadn't tried to kill some early spark that made you special. Now you can reignite it.

Breaking through the roadblocks can be scary. You're being asked to push yourself to achieve more than you've been brainwashed into thinking you could. But you have just as much potential as anybody to come out of the wings onto center stage. That's why Pluto is dragging you from your comfort zone. He's asking you to live your life fully—*your* way—without apologies or explanation to anyone.

Pluto also forces you to confront your own false humility. Anywhere Pluto travels, he churns up a craving for power. Even if you're the shyest person in your crowd, when Pluto and the Sun connect, you begin to feel destined for something better.

Shedding your timid side by daring to take a risk on yourself is part of the force operating within you. No, this isn't about becoming a self-centered egomaniac. That can be as disastrous for you as it was for Apollo when he insulted the wrong little cherub.

Apollo was the Sun god, and the world revolved around him. As Jupiter's son, he had power over everything, from music to medicine, and he was eternally young, handsome, and full of pride. His downfall came when he made fun of Cupid for carrying a bow and arrows. Apollo bragged about his skill as an archer and told the cherub to leave the weapons of warriors to those who knew how to use them.

While Apollo was browbeating the little guy, Cupid's friend Daphne, a gorgeous nymph, walked by. Cupid saw that Apollo liked her and decided to show him with whom he was messing. He took two arrows from his quiver. One was lead, which represented hate. The other was silver, representing love. Cupid shot Daphne with the lead arrow and sent the silver one straight into Apollo's heart.

Apollo fell on his knees and declared his eternal love to Daphne, who shrank back in disgust. She couldn't stand him—and he couldn't stand being without her. This hopeless mess ended when she begged her father (the river god, Ladon) to either let the Earth swallow her or change her appearance. He sadly agreed and turned her into a laurel tree, an evergreen in any season. Of course, this did nothing to end Apollo's suffering, and he swore to tend her forever, pledging that her leaves would decorate the heads of heroes and kings.

Apollo's tale demonstrates two of the dangers lurking in the fifth house—an overblown ego and fanatical love.

Love Affairs and Lusty Obsessions

While Pluto's meandering through your space, he turns up the heat in your bedroom. But unlike the long-term partnerships in the seventh house or the focus on marriage-type relationships in the eighth, these romantic ties aren't usually binding (unless you count who gets tied to the bed).

Fifth house romance is casual and flirty. Although long-term love is possible, the normal scenarios are short-term affairs and one-night stands. This is the house where you try on new lovers the way you'd try on a new pair of shoes. You like that one's style and this one's fit. Beware, though, when Pluto stands in your bedroom door, your love life can get messier than a rent-by-the-hour motel room.

If you're single, this could be one of the most interesting and fun times of your life—or it could be a time when you step away from romance for a while. The opposite of uninhibited sex is celibacy. Sometimes, this transit can make us tired of the game-playing and relationship dramas. You may decide to simply take a break from the love chaos. If you feel this way, this is the perfect time to step back and reassess why your love life is such a mess.

Another possibility is that you could find your first sweep-you-off-your-feet romance. Venus rules love, but Pluto rules passion. In the fifth house, Pluto can turn up the fire to boil your blood with desire.

If partnered—and if your relationship is tight—this journey can awaken those first-love feelings of excitement. It is a wonderful transit of renewal and spontaneity in your relationship. But sometimes this means you have to give up some kind of control you've had over your spouse or partner. Maybe you've been the one to say when and where more often, or you've used sex as a weapon. Yes, those scenes can occur at any time in life, but that kind of behavior totally negates sex as the joyful, shared experience it's meant to be. There's no room for selfishness in this *boudoir*.

The dark side of Pluto's passion is manipulation and obsession. Ego lives in the fifth house, and when ego and sex appeal mix, you may begin to believe you're not only irresistible but infallible. You could also run into someone who's all too willing to make you *their* next conquest.

Along with Neptune, Pluto is a planet of temptation. The difference is that Neptune gets seduced (by self-delusion) while Pluto is the seducer. During his tour of your sex life, Pluto enhances your ability to tempt or trap any poor soul you get the hots for, whether they're a stranger, an outlaw, or even your brother-in-law. He also lessens your ability to resist temptation, especially if your love life has been one disaster after another up to this point. Don't expect the same lust-'em-then-leave-'em routine, however. Where Pluto's concerned, the plot is thickened with revenge, betrayal, and danger.

Take a long look at your past relationships. Do you cling like moss to any loser who pays attention to you? Are you falling for the first person who strokes your ego? Are you trying to punish whoever crushed your self-image and your love by making another poor someone miserable? Facing the part you play in attracting destructive people starts the process of repairing both your self-esteem and your love life.

If partnered, you must beware of getting trapped into a casual fling. You might not get caught the first time or the second. But in the long run, Pluto always holds us accountable. So if you play, sooner or later, you will pay.

Wunderkind or Wannabe?

Potential lives in the fifth house. Boatloads of talent float around here, and whether they carry A-list superstars or F+ failures, all share a plain fact: potential means nothing without hard work. *Use it or lose it* is a cliché, but it's exactly what will happen if you don't get your butt in gear. Just like what happened to Beth.

Beth wanted to be a novelist, and when Pluto moved into her fifth house, he handed her a bagful of opportunities. She met Ellie, a published author and writing teacher, who became her mentor. Under her tutelage, Beth won a first-novel contest with publication as the prize—and the same small press published her second novel.

While Beth worked on her third book, she worked harder at cultivating Ellie's friendship. They went to writers' conferences, where

Beth mingled with well-known authors, agents, and editors. And upon Ellie's recommendation, Beth even landed a New York literary agent.

Sounds like a dream come true, doesn't it? Pluto had done everything but channel a bestseller for Beth, and her career seemed poised to blast into the stratosphere. Instead, it fizzled. She stalled because she didn't take control of her budding opportunity. After several months of increasing frustration and no progress, Beth left the group. She never wrote another book.

To her friends and family, she played the part of a successful writer. The truth was that she was afraid to take a risk on herself by pushing her craft to the next level. And she was too willing to let everyone else—especially Ellie—take responsibility for her success.

Pluto in the fifth house unleashes powerful creative impulses, awakening an all-or-nothing desire to succeed. With Pluto as the puppeteer, however, this intense energy can also get twisted into a desire to manipulate people and situations in order to get recognition and attention. Instead of doing the work herself, Beth leaned on others to do it for her.

Baby Face

Kids live in the fifth house, and one creative urge you may get is to have one. But before you *ooh* and *ah* over the possibility of a mini-you gurgling in her crib, you'd better stop and think about the lifelong responsibilities of parenthood.

Pluto drives passion, and passion drives creativity. Passion can also fog your head where having babies is concerned. The danger is becoming so obsessed with having a kid that you trap yourself and your partner into thinking that a baby will make things better. If you're considering this, it's time to wise up.

Susan's first marriage lasted less than six months. She got the car, furniture, and a baby girl. Although her ex paid child support, Susan had to rely on the extra money her parents gave her to make ends meet.

When Pluto moved into her fifth house, Susan decided to return to college. Her parents footed the bill and paid her living expenses, and her cousin moved in to care for the little girl in exchange for room and board. Susan seemed to be getting her life back on track.

Enter Josh. He was also divorced and had an eight-year-old daughter. Susan and Josh met at Christmas and he'd moved in by the end of January. He proposed on Valentine's Day. She said, "Yes, and by the way, I'm pregnant." So they eloped that night. Their newly wedded bliss lasted three days before their first fight. She slammed the bedroom door. He slept on the couch. The next battle ended up with her storming out of a store and disappearing into the night. Josh drove around for hours trying to find her, finally calling his parents, who lived in a neighboring town, to help in the search. Susan was fine, but the marriage was on the rocks before it started.

Susan's story is a classic example of fifth-house obsession and manipulation when Pluto's a houseguest. She'd decided she wanted Josh and that getting pregnant would seal the deal. After the lust-dust settled, however, she was stuck with a guy she barely knew and a baby conceived for all the wrong reasons. Her cousin left, and she and Josh are still breaking up and making up.

Everyone knows that children don't keep a relationship together. But during a Pluto transit, this advice should be tacked to your headboard.

Breaking the Pattern

Pluto's trip through your fifth house challenges you to release the inhibiting behaviors that prevent you from living a more joyful life. You could call this the life-is-a-banquet home. Your deepest need to express yourself as an individual in an unhindered way—without guilt or fear—is contained in this area.

Creation is a natural human urge. Although having children is one of the main themes, fifth-house creativity can include anything from renewing a neglected talent to starting a new hobby. Think about what interests you and experiment.

Love in the fifth house is flirtatious and mischievous. Yes, it can lead to a forever bond, but when Pluto's the matchmaker, you're required to confront your intentions and beware of the attentions of others. Before you leap, consider everyone's motivation.

Potential may drip from your fingertips, but without hard work, all the talent in the world isn't going to get you anywhere. The first rule of success is to sit your butt in the chair and do whatever it takes.

Having an ego often gets a bad rap, but a healthy self-image protects us from wet blankets and control freaks. It drives our ability to take a risk, survive our failures, and keep believing in ourselves. Wanting attention is a natural human desire, and nurturing your inner child helps rebuild the confidence you were born with.

Once you step out of the shadows of the faultfinders and fun-smothering grouches, you'll begin to see that your instinct for happiness hasn't disappeared. Then you'll not only help others to find their joy, you'll find yours too.

PLUTO IN THE SIXTH HOUSE

The Phoenix of Service

At a Glance: The Sixth House

This split-level abode has two focal points: health and everyday routine. Our day job and how we feel about it lives here. Are we workaholics or just clocking time until the weekend? Are we living a healthy or ticking-time-bomb lifestyle? In its evolution, the soul is learning how to get along with people on a professional basis and to care for the body we occupy.

The Inspector General

When Pluto strides into your sixth house, your everyday life, health, and work get the onceover. He demands that you face any negligence in these areas, and he'll twist your head around until you do. Ignoring problems here can have life altering consequences.

Mercury, the planet of half-truths and rationalization rules the sixth house. He also rules the Third House of Communication. However, in the sixth, he's grounded by Earth. And instead of dissecting everyone else's behavior, Mercury's microscope is focused inward, thanks to laser-eyed Pluto.

Mercury and Pluto know each other well. They're used to hashing out problems because Mercury was the only god that had the nerve to travel into Hades. He kept Pluto entertained by dishing the dirt from around the cosmos, and delivered messages between Pluto and the other gods. They connected in the Third House of Communication to push for honest talk, and they meet in the sixth to examine the details of daily routine. In this earthly environment, Pluto and Mercury make a good team. Pluto loves to probe, prod, and investigate while brainy Mercury becomes more focused. You get the best and the brunt of each.

The sixth house is the last of the self-focused houses. Here, the soul begins to learn how to be of service to others. Virgo owns this space, but before going further, let's set the record straight. Defining Virgo as the perfectionist of the zodiac is misleading. Though often portrayed as control freaks who never stop tweaking their worlds and ours, Virgo's intent is to offer helpful suggestions to make life easier. As Mutable Earth, Virgo strives to understand other points of view but gets nervous when the routine is altered. What the Virgin desires is organization and the security of a well-ordered life. Virgos need routine to flourish, and that's the core of the sixth house. No surprises, thank you.

When obsessive Pluto white-gloves this home, he uncovers the dirt that hides the cracks in your everyday life. Pluto isn't as willing to let self-neglect slide in this house. You're more likely to be forced to make the necessary changes than to exercise the free will you have during his other travels through your life. Think of this place as a tune-up shop. Physical checkups, lifestyle adjustments, self- or professional analysis, and refinement of job skills all exist here.

Count on facing the mistakes you've ignored and now must resolve. Lied or stretched the truth? Say hello to someone who bends the facts about you. Stuck in a job you hate? Pluto can drag office politics to a new low. Been careless with your health? You could get a scary wake-up call. Making excuses as to why you continue to put up with the boss from hell or push your luck with bad habits no longer works.

Emotional drama isn't a sixth-house trait. Your flaws get exposed as no-fuss facts, which can make you feel like a dimwit. But Pluto's purpose is to prove to you that you're capable of handling anything that life throws at you (and rest assured, he will toss plenty of irritating stuff your way). As with every Pluto transit, the challenges ebb and flow, but when the high tide rolls in through this door, the feeling is similar to living with Mercury in retrograde, only concentrated. There will be days or weeks when daily life spirals out of control. Maybe you make three lunch dates for the same day or three dinner dates for the same evening, with three people you met online. Your boss wants you to work overtime again. A friend needs to borrow your truck to help with moving. You have inch-long roots and your stylist left town. Soon, you're so overwhelmed that you forget to brush your teeth.

That's when the voice in your head starts quacking. *No matter how long you live, you will never do anything right.* This is your signal to stop listening to the tirade, which is also a routine—of self-defeat—and start investigating the source. Whose voice is it? As with everything, the way you approach the responsibilities of daily life began in childhood.

Pluto in your natal sixth house signals a lifelong struggle with the transition from kid to adult. In some way, your role models flopped in teaching you how to cope with the minutiae of day-to-day life. Maybe you never had to lift a finger at home because your mom was the family slave. Maybe you were the family slave in a group of irresponsible or abusive relatives—guilt, shame, and ridicule can be an ugly part of this scene. (*How can you be so dumb? What in the hell were you thinking?*) If any of these scenarios ring true, ask yourself how you think your childhood conditioning might affect your current everyday routine.

Another way to stop yourself from going bonkers is to consider how you fill your time. The sixth house is where everything should come together to make you a whole person. Duty to yourself and others, health, work, personal growth, relaxation—everything should be humming along in sync, at least most of the time. Is your day balanced? If not, where can you make adjustments? Time is a funny thing. The more you chase it, the less you have. When you slow down and work with it, you find all kinds of extra hours.

Pluto's arrival, either by birth or by transit, reveals the cracks and chips in this wheel. And repairing them requires finding the guidance you may not have received in childhood. Asking for help is the key. You may have to swallow some pride, and you will have to beware of phonies who wish to waste either your time or money. Start by observing the people you already know.

Is one of your office mates an organizational whiz who can help you stop the eternal paper shuffle? Does one of your friends or relatives know how to balance life's responsibilities with fun and self-indulgences? It won't be hard to find the help you need because Pluto is poised to send you a deluge of offers as soon as you ask—but you must take the first step.

Take This Job...

Pluto on the job creates power struggles. If you've suppressed your personal power in order to keep food on the table, you may be tempted to tell the boss to shove it as you shove off in search of more fulfilling work. That's the easy scenario. The wiser move is to send out your resume and wait for a better opportunity. Just make sure you're not exchanging one bad situation for another. The key to success is not repeating the same mistake.

Suppose you can't quit—the economy's tough. What then? With Pluto roaming through the workplace, you can bet he'll put the pressure on until you're forced to take a stand. The idea is to show you that working within other people's power structures is okay, up to a point. One of Pluto's missions is to help you learn how to do your best without sacrificing your personal power. If you've scattered your potential in a series of dead-end jobs, this transit is meant to focus your energy into a steady occupation. What interests you? That sounds like an easy question, but when you sit down and think about it, you might surprise yourself.

The flip side of this struggle is that if you've abused your power on the job, you're about to get decked. Not many of us walk through life observing our behavior patterns. Usually, it takes a shakeup to wake us up, and even that doesn't always work. Sometimes we have to get hit by the Pluto bus before we get wise.

Debra's standard on-the-job behavior was to criticize everything her coworkers did. She thought the way to impress her boss was to call attention to each minor rule infraction or error. As you can imagine, the boss became as frustrated with her as her coworkers were. Although a few of her complaints were legitimate, Debra had no idea how to fix them. And when the company had to downsize, guess who was included in the first round of layoffs?

Her next employer saw potential in Debra's commitment and gave her more responsibility, including a staff of three to supervise. Soon, her inner critic emerged and resumed its negative reinforcement pattern. After a series of confrontations with her team, Debra's supervisor days were over.

When you're so critical that people scatter when they see you coming, Pluto is trying to force you to examine why you feel the need to live in a perfect world. Where do you feel out of control? Who told you that making mistakes was bad?

In Debra's case, her grandmother was the culprit. When Debra's grandfather died, her parents brought her grandmother home to live with them. Grandma was a neat freak who policed the house like a hardnosed cop looking for a reason to bust anyone who made eye contact. Praise was something Debra rarely heard. *Hopeless Debra forgot to wipe her feet again. Clumsy Debra spilled her drink. Stupid Debra made the bed poorly.*

So, where were her parents? Working—and grateful to come home to a clean house and home-cooked meal every night. Besides, her mother had been subjected to the same rigid set of rules as a girl. She tried to make up for *her* mother's harshness by making excuses.

Many of us grow up in homes with strict rules and parents or relatives who strip our power with belittling remarks. The effects of this treatment play out in different ways, depending upon where Pluto is operating in our chart.

In the sixth house, the need for perfection can become obsessive. Thanks to her grandmother, Debra's message was that only perfect people were worthy of love. And Debra had to lose two jobs and face some hard facts before she could admit that she had many of her grandmother's heavy-handed traits.

Once she made the connection, Debra began to consciously work to control her critical judgments of others and not emotionally beat herself up over her own missteps. And she's making excellent progress. She has a new job and a chance for a promotion. Her coworkers are more receptive to her suggestions because her new attitude is nonthreatening, and she's learning to lighten up on herself as well.

When Pluto visits your sixth house, you might decide to start your own business. The lure of ditching a horrible boss or no longer having to work with a lazy louse can be very tempting—but be warned. You're about to get a crash course in the meaning of self-motivation. If you prove that you can stand the test of twice the work, all of the responsibility, and less money (at least at first), Pluto is prepared to help. Each step you take reinforces your ability to take care of yourself and develops your resourcefulness.

More than just deciding to become your own boss, you could find a whole new calling to which you want to dedicate your life. One of the ultimate objectives of the sixth house is to find meaning in your everyday work—a purpose that enhances your life as it enriches the lives of others.

Running the Show or Running in Circles?

Commonly called the House of Everyday Work, Service, and Health, one objective of the sixth house is to discover how well you manage your daily life. How productive do you feel? Is your to-do list longer than your arm? How well do you cope with the inevitable glitches that interrupt your routine? Are you so self-critical that you create further chaos? Or are you a control freak? Maybe you think you can fix all the problems of the world, starting with the grocery bagger who didn't properly pack your sacks.

No matter what, it's time to get real. When nothing goes right, Pluto asks you to look at what's going on behind the scenes in your life. Instead of assuming that the universe is dumping on you, it's time to find out what's making you feel and act like a failure. Who said that you were irresponsible or stupid? What happened that made you doubt yourself?

In the sixth house, Pluto demands that you do a lot of self-analysis. If you can't, he'll put the idea in your head that you might try therapy. No, you're not nuts. But it is irrational to stumble through life in a state of high anxiety. Self-help can be a big attraction when you begin to feel like you need to wear an *If found, return to* tag pinned to your shirt.

Alternately (or in addition to therapy), you may decide to read self-help books or seek out motivational gurus and programs. Just be careful of anyone who promises a quick fix. Pluto transits take years. You have time to make gradual and lasting progress. And because this transit is in the detail-oriented sixth house, you'll have the focus you need to make the commitment to discover why you're falling apart.

What Condition Is Your Condition In?

When Dr. Pluto appears, your years of hard partying start to show. Those sacks of fast-food tacos and extra martinis you poured down your throat return to haunt you. Blame your southern-fried child-hood or your spouse's love of saucy French cuisine if you want to. However, if you don't choose to correct the problem, Pluto will keep shoving those hush puppies and chocolate éclairs in your face until *you* have to face the consequences.

Bob was an overweight, chain-smoking internist who never prac-ticed what he preached to his patients. He self-medicated his high blood pressure, he "exercised" his elbow by grazing through office snacks all day and hoisting a few cocktails each evening, he foolishly thought he was the exception to the rule of healthy living. When Pluto moved into Bob's sixth house, Bob began exhibiting symptoms of early heart disease, but he ignored the infrequent bouts of chest pain as heartburn and chalked up his extreme tiredness to overwork.

One morning, Bob's office nurse arrived to find him collapsed on the floor of the waiting room. One triple bypass and thirty fewer pounds later, not only is Dr. Bob following his own advice, he's become an advocate of healthy living. Although he had to learn his

Pluto lesson the hard way, he's using his story to inspire others to change their lives.

While it is unlikely that you'll suffer such an ordeal to get your Pluto message, your body–mind–spirit connection will be under extra stress during this transit. Unresolved emotional issues could cause minor but nagging health problems to flare into chronic ailments. Have a pain in the neck? Figure out who makes you tense. Something gnawing at your gut? Try to identify the cause of your acid reflux. Overeating? Look into your soul to see what it's hungry for.

Pluto is an extremist, and you could swing from total neglect to total obsession concerning your health. *Caution*. This is not the time to suddenly start munching tree bark or to lay out thousands of dollars for a home gym. On the other hand, don't decide that you're gonna die anyway and stock up on double-meat pizzas with cheese-stuffed crusts.

What should you do? For starters, assess your lifestyle and begin to make wiser choices. Pluto's tour through your sixth house can inspire you to end harmful health habits. And regular physicals are mandatory, because serious health issues can also begin during this long-term transit and not show up until years later.

Finally, Pluto is the master of suspicion. So don't be surprised if you become skeptical of the medical profession—if you aren't already. You may decide that you can diagnose and treat yourself by googling your symptoms and researching the latest therapies. Or maybe you consider tossing out your blood pressure meds in favor of the latest alternative approach. Neither one is a good idea.

Although Pluto's trek through your medical file can help you to sniff out charlatans as well as cutting-edge medicine, the sixth house is about holistic/balanced living. No extremes allowed.

Breaking the Pattern

Healthy body. Healthy mind. Healthy spirit. Pluto's transit through the sixth house teaches us how to integrate these three powerful influences so that we can release the emotional poison that threatens to destroy our ability to function and thrive in our everyday world. Pluto's arrival signals that there's some work you need to do in one or more of these areas.

This journey is about solving the childhood issues that made you feel incapable of handling life's responsibilities or entitled to handing them over to someone else. To accomplish this goal will take a little help from your friends and/or a friendly counselor, and asking for that assistance won't be easy. Once you do, however, you'll find many people who are willing to share their time, advice, and expertise with you. Achieving a more balanced life requires patience and awareness, and Pluto's slow transit provides plenty of time for both.

Practice moderation in your lifestyle. All work and no play will turn you into a boring, mean robot (the stress will make you chronically irritable). If you're obsessively responsible, learning to hand off a few of your day-to-day responsibilities to your family will take practice. Make it easy and don't expect perfection. *Do* expect to have time to soak in a hot bath or have more Saturday afternoons to yourself.

Ask for help. People love to do two things: talk about themselves and give advice. During this transit, Pluto puts all kinds of helpful folks in your path. All you have to do is take the first step and be sincere.

Learn to fend for yourself. If you think the world owes you a living, you're about to get handed a pink slip. Personal growth means being aware of how your actions affect others. It's time to stop growing older and grow up.

Protect your body. Health is a major theme of the sixth house, and yours comes under Pluto's watchful eye. Regular checkups are a must, and so is eliminating harmful habits and undue stress. Strive for slow, steady progress. If you swing from one extreme to the other, you'll eventually crash.

The mind–body–spirit circle is the most important dynamic of a healthy life and healthy soul. Tend yours carefully. When you become aware of the effect your thoughts have on your body's health, you begin to break the downward spiral into stress-induced illness. You'll not only save yourself a headache, you may even save your life.

PLUTO IN THE SEVENTH HOUSE

The Phoenix of Partnership

At a Glance: The Seventh House

The Chapel o' Love is where the soul starts to expand its consciousness to include other people. Here, the soul begins the yin and yang of oppositions. The first house focuses on the self, but the seventh contains partnerships of all sorts. Think of this as the house we go to after graduation. We leave home and start to form other close relationships, including love. Are we after a joined-at-the-hip relationship, or are we serial romancers? Other partnerships influenced by the seventh house are best friends and business partners.

Buckle Up

You're about to take a ride on an emotional roller coaster of galactic proportions. Imagine one of those reality shows where the cast members live together in a huge mansion. They're searching for true love, best friends, or the perfect business partner. What they get is backstabbing, bed-hopping mayhem.

The seventh house contains most of your closest relationships. When Pluto moves in, you can expect at least a few episodes of trashy-novel drama. Going steady with Pluto is like hooking up with a midnight charmer who turns into creepy stalker at sunrise. You can escape a repeat performance, but you have to be willing to take a hard look at what you did to get yourself into the situation in the first place.

Venus, the goddess of love, rules this pad. Libra, the sign of justice, also calls the seventh house home. What's wrong with this picture of domestic tranquility? Venus's attributes may inspire poets, but she wasn't especially loyal to anyone but herself, despite her little-sexpot charm. Also, Libra's sense of justice can be a little lopsided. As long as the scales of partnership swing in its favor, Libra's a happy camper.

As in all Pluto transits, the underlying dysfunction is distorted truth. In the seventh house, the subject is intimacy. If you're born with this placement, unexpressed resentments within your family could have damaged your ability to trust. Living in a silent, tension-filled environment can be as unsettling as being in an openly hostile one. As a child, you felt the unspoken anger. Your parents brushed it off with a variety of excuses, and you learned not to trust your intuition or your judgment. Further, you learned that you couldn't trust the people closest to you.

Another distortion Pluto destroys is the unrealistic fantasy. Believing in the fairytale romance that ends in happily-ever-after perfection—or the idea that there's only one true love per customer—is just as damaging. So is being subjected to brutal or insensitive explanations about relationships. *All men cheat. All women try to trap you.* We've all heard them.

When Pluto transits your seventh house, situations designed to make you closely examine one or more of your tightest connections arise. Manipulation can be an issue—maybe your partner is trying to tell you how to dress, talk, and wear your hair. Or perhaps your business partner is attempting to persuade you into moving to a gorgeous but overbudget new office. In turn, think about ways in which you try to manipulate others. Those scales are supposed to balance your relationships, not get stacked in anyone's favor.

Intimate Strangers

We is the password to enter this domain. Although marriage and long-term love relationships dominate, these bonds include best friends, favorite relatives, business partners, and anyone else with whom you have a powerful connection. Call them soul mates. And yes, that term instantly conjures up the star-crossed lovers of fiction and movies—lovers who either go through hell and are reunited at the end, or go through hell and lose each other forever—but *real* soul mates include these scenarios and everything between.

We've all met someone that we feel we already know. We may have an instant attraction or repulsion to someone, and we've seen faces that are so familiar we stare at the person, trying to figure out who they are. These are soul connections too. When we form attachments to these people, they are always deep and compelling. What we don't think of when we imagine a soul mate is that, sometimes, the attachment is unhealthy.

Barbara's husband cheated on her for twenty years. Though she had threatened to divorce him more than once, he'd beg for forgiveness, she'd take him back, and they'd attend couples therapy every time. That was the pattern of their relationship.

Because of her distorted truth, she never learned how to handle the stress of his philandering. She even assumed some of the blame. Her job left her exhausted, the kids were hard to handle—who could blame him? The truth was that Barbara didn't kick his ass to the grass because she had learned the lie that women can't survive without men, and that marriage, even an emotionally abusive one, was better than being alone.

Barbara's health began to suffer. She developed panic attacks and high blood pressure. One evening, her closest friend invited her to dinner and confronted the issue. The friend suggested that Barbara see a therapist who could help her to free herself from this abusive situation. But Barbara felt betrayed and left.

That night, she couldn't sleep. Her husband was "working late" again. She got up and waited for him to stumble through the door. When he did, she told him to pack and leave—again. He did.

The next morning, Barbara called the friend and asked for the therapist's number. She's since filed for divorce and is learning to think about what is healthy for her before making *any* decision. In the past, Barbara didn't value herself enough to attract an emotionally valuable man.

As mentioned previously, every Pluto transit holds a meta-phorical mirror to your face. In the seventh house, you're asked to recognize where you're out of balance in your relationships. Think about how you handle them. Do you always develop infatuations with unavailable people? Say hello to the hot married guy who will never leave his wife, no matter what he whispers in your ear while you're doing the horizontal mambo. Or what about the gorgeous new coworker who, despite the ring on her finger, you set your sights on from day one?

Do you put your friends, business partners, and lovers on a pedestal then fall apart when they act like humans instead of heroes? Expect to discover just how human they can get. Or do you project wisdom and confidence, and come across as someone who can solve any problem? Prepare to meet someone who will expect you to do just that.

Maybe you're easy-going and have the glass-half-full perspective on life. You believe that as long as you think positively and treat others fairly, you'll be okay. Well, grab onto something, because Pluto is about to knock that fantasy out of your head. If you whine about how you can't find a decent partner but aren't tough enough to stand up for yourself, Pluto will keep on lining up the losers for your pleasure and pain. Perhaps your new best friend will borrow money you'll never see again, make a pass at your boyfriend, and then drunkenly puke on your favorite heels. And Pluto will make sure she also asks you to pick up the bar bill and let her crash at your place for the weekend.

The longer you avoid the truth, the more truth Pluto tosses in your face.

Love on a Merry-Go-Round

We told you a little of this tale back in the third house, The Phoenix of Truth section. Here's the rest of the story:

Passionate relationships can run amok when Pluto arrives. But this isn't entirely his fault. He learned about obsessive love through a rather nasty trick Venus played on him.

Venus was Cupid's mother. One day, when they were out snooping around Pluto's cave, she told the little cherub to aim an arrow at Pluto's heart. He did. Pluto instantly had a burning desire to come out of the dark and pursue the first hot body he saw. That happened to be Proserpina (Persephone), the beautiful daughter of his brother Jupiter. Despite the rift between them, Pluto begged Jupiter to let him have the girl, and Jupiter eventually did—partly because he knew Pluto's dark kingdom also held all the buried riches in the Earth. Old Greedy Gut thought he might get his hands on some of it in return for handing over his daughter. However, Jupiter's decision wreaked havoc. When Ceres, Jupiter's ex and Proserpina's mother, found out, she had a goddess-size meltdown. The Sun dimmed, and everything above ground froze and died. Winter had descended for the first time. Jupiter and Pluto were stunned by the force of Ceres's grief and, with Mercury handling the negotiations, agreed that Proserpina should spend half the year with Pluto in the dark realm of Hades and the other half with her mother on Earth.

Pluto rules sex and passion. When he rolls into your seventh house, he dives into your dark side and you can expect to have a few disturbing moments. You might meet a person to whom you're instantly, can't-wait-to-rip-their-clothes-off attracted. How you handle the situation is up to you, but be warned, falling into the arms of a fantasy lover—no matter how hot the sex is—is rarely the solution and rather a symptom of something that's gone wrong. You may even leave your spouse or partner and move in with your new Miss or Mr. Perfect. That definitely won't fix anything. The person you think is your cure-all is really only the Band-Aid lover. Soon, you'll have to peel this one off just as you've done the others.

Eternally playing the field or playing around is just as dangerous. This avoidance mechanism clicks into place when we refuse to accept the inevitable give and take that commitment requires. Jumping into bed but not getting involved, or cramming your social calendar so that you and your partner have no time to breathe, let alone think about problems—all such behavior is likely to destroy your bond permanently.

Candice was the queen of shallow relationships. Married and divorced twice, she had cheated on both her husbands—but they'd done the same to her, so she had no guilt. She dated single and married men alike, and took zero responsibility for her participation in the married guys' adultery. Her reasoning? They made the choice to cheat, so it was their problem, not hers.

Over the course of ten years, Candice had an ongoing affair with her married boss and a couple of flings with coworkers. She also had a few short-term relationships with single men. These were short-term largely because she couldn't commit past the lust stage, and she expected the guys to rescue her on a regular basis. Her Pluto come-uppance happened on several levels.

Her best friend of ten years told Candice that she and her husband had decided to try to spice up their love life by dating other people. At first, Candice seemed shocked by the revelation, but her friend insisted it was better than therapy. Then she said that her husband suggested that maybe Candice would like to meet him for a romantic evening. Candice was appalled by the thought of sleeping with her best friend's husband, no matter how open their marriage was. Her friend laughed, but Candice noticed that she also seemed relieved.

Then the rationalizations kicked in. He was cute, and her friend had brought up the subject. If she'd had reservations, she wouldn't have mentioned it in the first place, right? Soon, Candice and the husband had a tryst at a local hotel. And soon after that, her friend and the husband divorced. No surprise to Candice—their marriage had been over for a long time.

What blindsided Candice was that her closest friendship was also lost. Although she had noticed a change in her friend's behavior, she attributed it to the turmoil of going through the divorce. After the husband moved out, the friend continued to distance herself from Candice, finally cutting off all contact. Whether or not Candice made the connection that her friend considered the tryst with her husband an ugly betrayal that ruined their friendship, Candice acted as if she herself was the hurt party.

Next, the on-again-off-again affair with Candice's boss heated up to the point that he was spending as much time as possible with her. He talked of divorcing his wife. She assumed he meant he wanted to marry her, so she began making plans. He began backing off. When he did leave his wife, he didn't rush to Candice. He didn't even tell her. And after a few drama-filled confrontations, he dumped her.

Still stuck up to her eyeballs in denial, Candice first assumed the role of victim, then shook it off and tried to resume her party life. One by one, her other friends began to turn down her invitations and not include her in their plans. The ones that had relationships didn't trust her, and the men she'd bedded were tired of her high-maintenance style.

All of Candice's relationships had to hit bottom before she finally began to accept some responsibility for her part in these disasters. Her distorted truth was a deep fear of commitment that began when her college sweetheart died in an auto accident. Unconsciously, she equated real love with total loss.

Her pattern changed when she made the connection. Then the transformational power of her Pluto transit began. She quit her job and apologized to her ex-best friend, she made new friends, and no longer dates unavailable men.

When Pluto arrives, there's no more sidestepping your dark side. You will have to either face the issues or face the music. Unless you work out your internal issues, you'll repeat the same problems. Of course you shouldn't stay in an unworkable situation. However, if you keep running from bad relationships before figuring out your part in their destruction, Pluto will just follow in a U-Haul stuffed with your old emotional baggage. Sooner or later, he'll dump it into your new life.

Another seventh-house test Pluto creates is the compulsive need to be in a relationship—any relationship. Maybe your parents or other authority figures were control freaks. Prepare to meet a few more. Your best friend demands all your spare time and gets jealous if you hang with your other pals, and your new lover turns out to be as obsessive as the last three you lived with. Your business partner starts treating you like a clerk instead of an equal. On the other hand, if you have any of these nasty traits yourself, prepare for a Pluto jolt from the people you've used.

All of these situations have a common denominator—you. See if you can determine what motivates your actions. Do you need to be needed? Do you like being rescued? Are you afraid to be yourself because others might not love the real you? Now is the time to think about what you're doing to attract these lose-lose connections.

Even if your marriage, friendship, or business bonds are tight, chances are you'll have a few tense moments while Pluto works his will on your relationships. These bumps are intended to rattle your connection to see how strong it is. The good news is that these are the years in which you can grow closer and learn to work together to purge what doesn't mesh.

Some of us get a power surge of confidence when Pluto lands in the seventh house. Perhaps we've done our homework and are mindful (most of the time) of what we're doing. When this happens, we project such a force field of confidence and charisma that we can attract strong partners who match our poise and self-reliance. When we value our social and private relationships, we're valued too.

Love on Your Own Terms

Pluto's tour can also free you from guilt about whom and how you love.

Scott and his sister were raised in a strict, ultra-traditional family. Dad was the boss. Mom was the caregiver. And both were self-conscious about discussing the facts of life let alone anything outside a "normal" family life. To them, family meant marriage and children.

During high school, Scott's lack of interest in girls was chalked up to his shyness. In college, his father joked about him playing the field. After college, the jokes turned to pressure to find a nice girl and settle down. So Scott got married, and he appeared to be very much in love with his bride. Twenty years and one daughter later, Scott heard the tread of another pair of feet in the house. Pluto had arrived, and shook his life to its foundation. Pulling the strings behind the scenes, Pluto flipped on the floodlights in Scott's seventh house. As Scott sweated, Pluto increased the wattage and waited.

Scott had managed to keep up his happy-family-man act while his daughter was growing up. When she left for college, he finally acknowledged he'd been living a lie and told his wife that he was gay. He'd been experimenting with strangers while hiding his secret from her and his family. Although she was hurt, she wasn't as surprised as he'd expected. His wife had suspected the truth but chose to ignore it because it was easier to pretend the fairytale than face divorce and family scandal.

Out of guilt and shame, Scott had done what his parents had expected because he thought they would never accept a gay son. You bet it was hurtful to everyone involved, and it took intense family counseling to mend the pain. However, the pressure of hiding his true feelings made him so miserable he had to face the truth no matter what the outcome.

Today, Scott's parents and daughter accept him as his real self, and he's still friends with his ex-wife, who has remarried. He's also happily in love with an adoring partner.

Your trip may not be as traumatic, but this journey's purpose is to help you form strong, healthy relationships based on honesty, respect, and trust—relationships in which you're allowed to be who you are without reservation or fear.

Breaking the Pattern

The seventh house holds the promise of forming or strengthening lasting relationships that will sustain us through our lifetime. Opening your deepest self to another human being can be terrifying, and facing your shadow self through your relationships is grueling.

In business, you become partners by sharing responsibility without blame and success with equality. Friendship deepens through a slow exchange of information. Revealing your fears and sharing secrets creates trust. Though romantic love hits like a freight train, it requires nothing but chemical attraction. True intimacy takes absolute trust—and time.

This house is ruled by an Air sign, and Air communicates. Begin by talking to yourself. *What do I want?* Try to recognize the pattern that prevents you from getting it. Talk to the people you care about as well as potential partners, and don't be afraid to probe beneath the surface. Balance what you expect to receive with what you're willing to give.

When you work with your inner power—the force Pluto awakens during this transit—you learn that sacrificing yourself isn't always the best thing to do. Neither is making others sacrifice for you. You learn how to maintain your individuality while supporting your relationships. When you take responsibility for your part in creating unhealthy partnerships, Pluto shows you how to let go of unworkable situations and form healthy attachments. That's when you discover you can change—that you deserve to be loved and respected. And once you do, you'll begin to love yourself again.

PLUTO IN THE EIGHTH HOUSE

The Phoenix of Legacy

At a Glance: The Eighth House

Call this house the lawyer's office. Other people's possessions, inheritances, death, and sex live in the eighth house. Opposing the Second House of Money and Values (home to the money we earn and our personal values), the eighth house represents what others bring to or take from us. Legally binding contracts such as wills, marriage licenses, and pre-nup agreements are a part of this house. Emotional legacies from our ancestors are here. Mortgages, taxes, loans, and anything to do with what we owe to, receive, or want from others—and how we go about trying to obtain those things—are in the eighth house.

Dark Shadows

The scene changes in the eighth house. Instead of Pluto arriving on the doorstep, you knock on this door and he answers. The eighth house is Pluto's home on the zodiac wheel. When he yanks you across the threshold, you're on his turf, and that pleasant smile you show to the rest of the world fades as he begins to materialize the ghosts of your past.

The Romans never said Pluto's name aloud for fear that he would show up. He ferried the dead across the River Styx (the mythological border between Earth and the underworld) and into his realm of Hades. And once you were there, you didn't come back. However, this land wasn't the hell and damnation of eternal fire as portrayed in some religions.

Peaceful and pleasant areas also covered this landscape. The Elysian Fields were where the souls of heroes and honorable people went. The Asphodel Meadow held the souls of average people who had led mostly normal lives. Only those souls who had broken divine law or really irked Jupiter were sent into the darkest regions to dwell in isolation and suffering.

Rivers also ran through this setting. The most famous was the River Lethe, or "Oblivion." If you sat beside its banks, all memories of both the pleasures and pain of your life would be forgotten.

The eighth house is called the House of Shared Resources, Sex, and Inheritance. Eighth-house sex can be a head game of manipulation and punishment. There may be hidden sexual secrets or physical sexual problems. Shared resources are what your marriage partner or long-term lover brings to your union—money, debt, inheritances. Money you obtain from business partnerships is here as well.

Loss through a literal death of someone you know can happen anywhere Pluto roams, including during an eighth-house transit. However, the "death" you're more likely to experience is twofold. The first is a sense of losing everything or wanting to give up on some level because life can seem harder than ever during this trip. The second is your ability to find the strength to kill your self-destructive habits and behaviors.

When Pluto inhabits your eighth house by birth, or when you step into it during your transit, some of the issues you may face can feel like a trip to hell. Pluto's mission in any area of life is to destroy what doesn't work and transform the rubble into a stronger, more productive design. Here, he tackles some of your deepest and most sensitive areas.

Scorpio lives here too. Its symbol, the Scorpion, may be scary to look at, but it's mostly a harmless creature that will actually sting itself to death when cornered. Self-destruction may be the only way out for the scorpion, but we humans always have choices. One of them is to rise from the ashes of our destructive urges or the destruction that others have tried to force on us, which illustrates another of Scorpio's symbols, the Phoenix. This magical bird represents the cycle of rebirth from death—exactly the intention of your eighth-house Pluto transit.

Legacies

Secretly wishing that Gramps will kick off and leave you enough dough to climb out of debt? He may croak, but you might have to fight his new wife for your share of the loot. In fact, the scuffles can get so dirty that you could end up wrestling your siblings for the Tupperware.

Family legal battles over money and possessions can reach epic proportions. Betrayal and underhanded attempts to push you out of the picture are common.

Evelyn's parents died in an airplane crash when she was a freshman in college. While she was reeling from the shock, her two much-older sisters were maneuvering behind her back to get copies of the will and haul as much of their parents' personal property out of the house as they could manage. All Evelyn wanted was their support and comfort.

In this case, Pluto stepped in by sending Evelyn a tough advocate in the family lawyer who put a stop to the sisters' creeping the family mansion. But the battles had just begun. The will left half of the estate to Evelyn and 25 percent to a variety of environmental causes. The big sisters got to split the other 25 percent.

Maybe it sounds like Mom and Dad didn't like their oldest children, but the truth is that they had given each of their elder daughters a liberal trust fund, college educations, and generous cash gifts. They'd also set up college funds for their three grandchildren. Both women were financially comfortable professionals married to financially stable men.

Evelyn's parents chose to safeguard her by ensuring that she had enough money to finish school and give her a good start in life. Of course, the sisters contested the will, but they lost. Pluto had protected Evelyn from their attempts to steal her inheritance.

On the other side of that coin, is the story of Jess. His father left a modest insurance policy to cover his final expenses and give each of his sons a small inheritance.

Jess had talked Dad into listing him as sole beneficiary with the promise that he would settle the bills and send his brother, who lived in another state, his half of the remainder. His brother, Charlie, knew and approved of the arrangement because he trusted Jess.

After the funeral, Charlie went home and Jess applied for the insurance money. He paid his dad's funeral costs and final medical bills, then sent Charlie a check for $500. It should have been $5,000.

Charlie learned the truth when he returned to pick up some of his father's personal items a couple of months later. While sorting through the paperwork in his dad's desk, he discovered a stack of receipts and did the math. When confronted, Jess burst into an angry tirade. He confessed he kept the money, yelling that he deserved it because he was the one who had gotten stuck living closer to their dad in his old age.

Charlie didn't fight over the lost cash. Instead, he went home with the mementos he'd chosen. But his brother's betrayal had shocked him. Further, Jess's outburst had made Charlie feel both guilty and angry. As time passed, the division between them widened, and today, they rarely speak.

Evelyn's grief for her parents pushed any thought of money out of her mind and Pluto helped her keep what was rightfully hers. Jess got an extra $4,500 of the insurance money but lost his relationship with his brother in the process.

Greed is one of the eighth house's worst monsters, and Pluto masterminds plenty of temptation to see whether you'll let it run wild. Even if you're innocent, you could still end up in a fight for what's yours. During this transit, Pluto may test your ethics in dealing with inherited money as well as assets you share with personal and business partners. Would you pass?

Other legacy challenges you may have to deal with are the emotional ones you received from family members, your ex, or anyone who has hurt you, as Pluto reanimates old wounds you've tried to forget.

Buried pain doesn't go away. Like a rotting corpse, it festers and contaminates everything around it. You might be shocked at the force of your emotions when a hurtful memory bubbles up, because the pain can seem just as raw today as when it first occurred. So, what do you do? Shake it off and tell yourself that you're over it? Feel guilty because the person who hurt you is dead and you shouldn't harbor a grudge anymore?

When these traumas rise like specters in your head, you must admit that you do still hold a grudge, want revenge, or hate the person. Pluto demands truth wherever he goes. Trying to *be bigger than the other person or forgive and forget* won't work in Pluto's house. You may have paid lip service to these concepts because that's what was expected, but you might also like to have the chance to get even. This trip is all about learning how to accept your own dark side without judging yourself.

Venting your anger after years of swallowing it is a good way to clear the air. It's honest and direct. And you don't have to scream or start a brawl. Sometimes, a simple phone call will do. You just have to acknowledge your true feelings.

If you don't think you can stand the conflict or if your enemy is no longer in the picture, then talk to one of your Pluto-type friends or family members. These are the people in your life who possess the power to express their feelings by saying exactly what's on their mind. He or she will understand the deep resentment or disgust you feel, and you'll have a safe way to unleash your fury.

Other People's Money

The eighth house is a money house, similar to the Second House of Money and Values. However, the focus is on other people's money and how it affects you through marriage, business partnerships, or close relationships. Sharing these monetary and material resources— or the lack of them—can be harder than you think.

Does money motivate your love, or do you think you can live on love alone? Pluto exposes both of these extremes. Maybe you marry a big spender and wake up in bankruptcy court. You might fall for a sweetheart who's looking for the right career and, ten years later, you're still working two jobs to make ends meet.

Maybe you hook up with someone who uses money to blackmail and control you or your family members. Or a relative may be scheming behind the scenes to take charge of the family finances. You might not find out that you've been manipulated until it's too late. On the other hand, if you're the manipulator, prepare to get publicly steamrolled. Exposing your faults is Pluto's job. Repairing the damage is yours.

Marilyn had money and married more. She invested her money in her husband's business empire, and together they've made an even bigger fortune. During their fifteen-year marriage, they've had three children, and though Marilyn's husband has never been faithful, she's chosen to ignore it because of the high-profile life she loves. She and her husband rarely see each other, and sex (as well as any other intimacy between them) is nonexistent.

Take a casual glance at Marilyn's life and it looks idyllic. But she's chosen to tie herself to a loveless relationship in exchange for a materially fat world.

In contrast, when Pluto invited Sam into his domain, all the trouble in his failing marriage erupted like Mount Saint Helens. The more Sam earned, the more his wife spent. Although she worked, he worked overtime and picked up extra money on the weekends as a handyman to pay for new cars, vacations, and her pseudo-rich-bitch lifestyle. Nothing he tried worked, including marriage counseling. Sam believed that money was a means to an end. His wife believed money made her better than everyone else.

As Pluto applied the pressure, Sam saw his life unfolding as a never-ending jog around the cash-cow treadmill. He confronted his wife, and they fought for days. Finally, he gave her an ultimatum, "Cut back, or I leave." He left, and filed for divorce.

An eighth-house divorce can be especially ugly, because greed often overshadows the process. But Sam wanted out and didn't care what it cost financially. Even though his wife had her own income and they had no children, in exchange for a quick divorce, Sam gave his wife the house, car, and a cash settlement. The bright side is that dangling a check at a money glutton is like tossing a tuna to a shark. It gets their attention long enough to allow you to escape.

On the happier side, this can be a wonderful transit for boosting your income through alliances with key people who invest money in you or your ideas and who support and believe in you. Meeting powerful people during these years can help you become a money-making machine. Just make sure that your idea of getting rich doesn't involve a pyramid scheme or becoming a collection agent on commission for the mob.

If you're already in business, it's time for a self-check of whether you are picking up your end of the partnership. Are you sharing the responsibility fairly? Have you been slacking off and letting your partners do all the work while still expecting your fair share of the profits? Or maybe you're getting taken advantage of. Cheating of any kind gets exposed under Pluto's watchful eye.

On a broader scale, you may run into frustrating problems or get pleasant and unexpected surprises from impersonal entities. Banks and mortgage companies may make it harder to get a loan. Or you might be suddenly handed a chance to reduce your interest rate. Also, taxes are represented in this house. If you're audited, you'd better have a whistle-clean return. Otherwise, the penalties and fines will be worse than if you're caught cheating during any other Pluto transit. Even if you've made an honest mistake or the Feds have screwed up your paperwork, you can still have a nightmare on your hands. Last but not at all least, scam artists run through the eighth house just as they do in the Second House of Money and Values. The difference is that the scam is larger and more intricate and, if you fall for it, can wipe you out.

Money is the root of all evil is not exactly precise. The correct quote is, *For the love of money is the root of all kinds of evil.* The key word is *love*. How much do you love money? What would you be willing to do to get it?

Fire or Ice

Sex lives in the eighth house. Although sexual issues can arise in any house that Pluto visits, when he comes home, he brings a trunk full of toys and erotic obsessions. Don't freak if you start having fantasies about the bag boy at the grocery store or the bag lady on the corner. Your thoughts are neither bad nor good. Only your actions count. Pluto is an obsessive guy, and when touring your eighth house, sexual misadventures can crop up all over town.

Unresolved problems from Pluto's tour in your Seventh House of Partnerships get distilled into sexual warfare. Control is the focus. Hidden sex is the danger. If you've been pointing your toes at the ceiling in your lover's bedroom, your spouse or partner is more likely to find out when you're in Pluto's house.

Using sex as a weapon becomes tempting, especially with control-freak Pluto sharing the bed. But withholding sex to punish or manipulate is a game you won't win. Neither will pressuring your partner to have sex when he or she isn't in the mood.

How do you feel about your partner? Do you wish he or she was more aggressive? Less? Sexier? Dead? What are you willing to do to rekindle the passion? If so, consider your options, then talk to your partner. Communication is crucial. Whether you can initiate the conversation yourself or need guidance from a therapist, making the first move will tell the one you love that you're at least willing to try.

What if you're single? Sex will still be in focus, as the eighth house encourages experimenting and learning about sexual relationships. However, in today's world, where making love can kill and predators lurk, irresponsible sex just can't happen. That doesn't mean you have to check into the local convent, but you do have to exercise both common sense and caution.

Affairs with emotionally or practically unavailable people may be very appealing—and not just because you get the hots for someone's marital tale of woe. Having secrets of any kind can be fascinating obsessions during this transit. What a luscious and naughty thing a hidden tryst becomes. But if you have to be told that having these secrets is certain to end badly, you haven't done your Pluto homework.

The Hall of Mirrors

Imagine a long, narrow room lined with paintings of faces. The place is full of shadows and the paintings are dusty—you have to get really close before you can recognize the portrait. And when you wipe the dust away and peer into the frame, you discover these aren't paintings at all—they're mirrors. Each one exposes a flawed version of yourself.

There's a saying that behaviors we can't stand in others are often reflections of our own bad behavior that we don't recognize. What are some traits you see in others that annoy the hell out of you? Can you think of times when you've acted the same way? Some of these behaviors also reflect one or more of our weaknesses—things we may feel guilty about or try to hide because we were taught that they are bad or cowardly.

When you walk down Pluto's hallway, these characters begin to step out of the mirrors and into your life. Do you have trouble taking responsibility? Prepare to meet the world's champion flake. Team up with this loser and you'll instantly double your load, because she'll have broken her toe or put out an eye to avoid pulling her weight. Are you a procrastinator? Say hello to the guy who's never met a deadline in his life. Do you walk around like a cat with its back up, bristling for a fight? You'll run into a rude or thoughtless person on every corner.

Don't close your eyes, because you can't avoid these deadheads. Each one represents something in you that needs to be acknowledged then let go, including guilt about your darker feelings. In the eighth house, reclaiming your personal power means recognizing that even when dark thoughts and desires bubble to the surface, thoughts are neutral. Only your actions count.

If you've been a perpetual doormat, you're here to learn a power word—no. Pluto asks you to fight hard for yourself without resorting to cutthroat tactics. Sure, he's the last one to be pointing fingers about sneaky dealings, but he's not the one who must evolve. You are.

Breaking the Pattern

Your visit to Pluto's home challenges you to root out and destroy as many dark emotions as possible. Revenge, guilt, fear, greed—this house is filled with passions that can destroy you. And coming face to face with your own versions of these demons will be intense. To survive, you must be honest with yourself.

Look at the emotional legacies you've received from your family. Think about the one you're creating in your lifetime. Try to recognize your flaws in the people who push your buttons, then pinpoint why they're so irritating. Think of when you acted the same way. Share the wealth of your spiritual as well as material resources. Renew the passion in your relationships by letting your guard down and speaking from your heart.

When you admit you have a dark side, you can begin to eliminate the power it holds over you and diminish the power of those who would control you. Once you do, the mirrors in Pluto's dark hall shatter and your light begins to shine.

PLUTO IN THE NINTH HOUSE

The Phoenix of Belief

At a Glance: The Ninth House

The public relations firm is home to higher education of the mass-market kind. The third house bestows a silver tongue. The ninth house expands it to include philosophical discussion and plenty of advice (which is not always dispensed with tact and diplomacy). Astrology and religion share space in this dwelling, as do publishing, long-distance communication, and world travel. The soul's mission here is to look for meaning through understanding other cultures and belief systems.

The Information Highway

Your karma is about to eat your dogma. In the ninth house, Pluto becomes the hit man who slays your self-righteous beliefs.

The ninth house exists to expand your mind. Ruled by Jupiter, big boss of the universe, this is the House of Philosophy, Travel, and Knowledge. Think of a huge library that's open 24/7 and full of people who are all talking at once about everything, from the meaning of life to the probability of being abducted by aliens. Now picture Pluto slamming through the double doors, boot heels cracking on the hardwood as he marches into the center of the room. Heads snap up. Conversation stops. *WTF?*

Why would he disturb these discussions? Because everyone is talking and no one is listening—that's Jupiter's influence. He talked all the time because his word was law. Ninth-house conversations can sound like you and the other person are reading aloud from two different novels. You're making lots of noise but neither hears what the other is saying.

As warm and friendly as its Mutable-Fire Element, Sagittarius hangs out in this space. Its symbol, the Archer, is a centaur (half man, half horse) who carries a bow and arrow representing the search for knowledge. Like the centaur, Sagittarius roams through the world collecting stories and telling new-and-improved versions to anyone it can corner.

Jupiter, Sagittarius's ruler, was always free to go anywhere and say anything he pleased, and even if someone didn't quite buy what he was selling, they didn't dare disagree. Reclusive Pluto was Jupiter's brother, but Pluto was stuck in the underworld, guarding the dead so they couldn't zombie around outside. Imagine how sick Pluto was of having to sit through Jupiter's endless stream of consciousness. Pluto wants the real truth, not Jupiter's expanded version. When he moves into his brother's house, he brings a big dose of *prove it to me* with him. And when he moves into your ninth house, you may start questioning the rhetoric you've heard all your life too.

My God's Bigger than Your God

Religion is one of the main themes in the ninth house. The library represents your curiosity about what people think and believe outside your backyard and hometown. However, its base of knowledge is the information you learned from whoever raised you. And the perceptions you bring to your discussions are ones you've built upon this basic information dump.

When Pluto comes around, he rattles the foundations of these belief systems that have been passed on as the only truth in your life. Benevolent god. Vengeful god. No god. His goal is to help you break away from these absolutes and open your mind to different concepts so that you find your own truth.

At the beginning of Pluto's visit to her ninth house, Arianna's frustration with her mother's rigid views exploded.

"I don't know how to explain it, but everything just feels different," she said. "Why should our religion be better than someone else's?"

The tension with her mother had started when she took a world religions class at school. When Arianna attempted to discuss what she was learning, her mother would cut her off or warn her she was "playing the Devil's game." Arianna's solution was to try to keep the peace at home by not discussing the subject, but she refused to drop the class. Though her mother still worries about her soul, Arianna continues to expand her knowledge about other belief systems.

This story is an all-too-frequent example of how severe religious rules generate fear. Arianna's mother is convinced that her way is the one true way, but Arianna's Pluto transit pushes her to evolve by learning there are many spiritual paths. This transit can turn a mild curiosity into the obsession to find the meaning of life. Arianna's statement that everything felt different is typical as Pluto prods you to step beyond the boundaries of fear and superstition.

Ruth abandoned her religious beliefs in her twenties. For a while, she attended a variety of traditional and nondenominational churches, but she eventually stopped going altogether. When Pluto entered her ninth house, she began to seek spiritual guidance again and ended up back where she'd started, within the religion of her childhood.

Pluto's trek through your ninth house is not a protest against religion or an attempt to destroy what you or anyone else believes. Its purpose is to make you question those all-encompassing concepts that provide simplistic answers to the deep, eternal mysteries of the universe and all of creation.

Ninth-house energy is idealistic. Humanity at its highest potential of enlightenment lives here. There's no room for hell-and-damnation sermons or rigid moral rules. We've all seen the horrific results of religious fanaticism as well as spiritually damaging acts of ostracism, hate crimes, and intolerance.

There's also no room for total objectivity. Maybe you take a scientific approach to answering the whys of life. Introducing a little take-some-things-on-faith subjectivity into your belief system can steer you closer to your personal path to enlightenment.

Whether it's the Bible Belt Bus of Eternal Bliss or the DNA Rocket to the God Gene, or another spiritual information highway you travel, when Pluto hops a ride, he tosses the road map out the window. The more open minded you are, the easier this trip will be.

If you were born with a ninth-house Pluto, you most likely grew up with the religion of your family. You probably followed one of the major organized religions, practiced one of the more than four thousand other recorded ways to commune with your higher power, or were taught that education or politics or money was the only creed you needed.

Every religious tome was passed by word of mouth for hundreds of years before being written down. Remember the game Telephone? If a sentence can't get through a circle of six or eight people without becoming more fiction than truth, why should you think and believe that any spiritual word that's been filtered through the human ego for centuries is accurate? Similarly, plenty of self-aggrandizing know-it-alls can float through your life during this trip. And *all* of them will offer you the secret of eternal life as defined by their religious or spiritual beliefs.

Whatever your family believed or didn't believe in, everyone knew the family views. And maybe you knew it was mostly bull droppings. Maybe you were born questioning anything that restricted you to one way of life or stifled the questions that flooded your mind. Maybe your parents followed a lacquer-haired TV evangelist who was later caught with both hands in the collection plate. You could have had more than an average number of associations or encounters with hypocrites—the bigoted religious leader, the morally delinquent caregiver. Whatever happened, chances are that you grew up with a cynic's eye. Has skepticism become your belief system?

If you chose the opposite of your family's beliefs, it's possible you continue to fear or distrust everyone who doesn't fit your current mold. Perhaps you're still power tripping over those whom you consider less enlightened.

None of these extremes are acceptable. In your heart, you may feel that nothing fits, you're missing a crucial fact but don't know how to find it. If so, try to ask questions. Read about other belief systems on the internet or by checking out books about religion or philosophy at the library. Talk—and listen—to people with different belief systems. And do it without prejudice.

Tripping Through the Universe

Another ninth-house subject is long-distance travel. Commonly, these journeys are described as physical trips around the country or the world—study programs or vacations to a foreign country. Although you may decide to take that vacation to Singapore, the purpose of any journey during Pluto's trip through this home is to cultivate an appreciation for other cultures and to enlighten your spirit.

Stan's ninth-house transit coincided with his retirement. The last couple of years he worked, he took some online history courses. After retirement, he and his wife visited a few of the places he'd studied.

Nancy's Pluto journey began while she was in college, and the travel bug hit her hard. She became an exchange student and lived in Spain for a year.

Marta moved from the freewheeling United States to work in a Muslim-dominated country for two years. The culture shock was both intimidating and inspiring.

You don't have to travel around the world to trip through the universe with Pluto. This transit can help you break free of a simple Sunday-and-sports rut by deciding to take a drive with your family instead of sitting in front of the TV. Maybe you decide to start walking around your neighborhood more or you take more long weekends to visit a favorite getaway spot.

Never Stop Learning

When Pluto's probing energy emerges, you may feel uneasy about the curiosity that bubbles through your mind. *Is there life on other planets? Life after death? Who knows?* Embrace your uneasiness. The more you question, the more you'll learn. More important, you'll connect with other people who aren't afraid to crash through the die-hard barriers of platitudes designed to control humanity through fear and superstition.

Although Jupiter's feel-good energy rules the ninth house, wherever Pluto steps, he leaves muddy footprints. The dark side of his trek through the land of enlightenment is that he tempts your need to do a little fact twisting. The ninth house is one of the most important areas in life because its ideal is to work for the collective good. Though the eleventh house also rules a collective ideal, it emerges on a personal level. The energy in the ninth can work on a global scale.

Pluto is obsessive about finding the truth—remember how he was fed up with Jupiter's incessant blather? One way you can sabotage the inspirational values you're supposed to learn is by falling under Jupiter's spell of desiring to spread your word and only your word. Don't become one of those charming con artists who spreads their lies with a smile. Never believe that you have found the one true answer to anything. That's a red light that you're in danger of creating your own god complex—and the perfect way to receive a karmic ass-kicking from you know who.

If you dropped out of school, you might desire to complete your education. Maybe you'll have the urge to also get a higher degree. You could decide to focus on one topic and not worry about formal education. If classrooms and campuses don't appeal to you, there's a world of knowledge at your fingertips through the internet. And if that isn't your cup of tea, try picking up a novel or nonfiction book, or try your hand at writing. One of the lesser themes of the ninth house is the written word. Who knows? Maybe you'll write the next international bestseller.

A Higher Purpose

Whether you were born with Pluto in the ninth house or are living the transit, you're one who has a chance to bring people together for the sake of humanity. While you may not want to operate on the world's stage or become a TV guru, you will have the ability to influence people around you to open their minds to investigate beyond their own belief systems. You can free them of the guilt of doubt and the fear of questioning.

Our Earth is the only speck of life in the known universe. Whether or not life exists elsewhere is a mystery we'll never discover until we take that journey. And whether life after death exists depends on your personal perspective. Every question you ask and every open-minded conversation you have about the mysteries of creation and the philosophies of religious or spiritual beliefs moves you one step closer to truth.

Those who would keep you under their thumbs don't want you to question anything. When Pluto moves into your ninth house, however, he demands that you do. He makes sure that you become aware of the power and abuses of blind faith. If you are already aware, that's great. You'll have an advantage as you meet people who are scarily intense about their convictions. You might become intrigued by what you hear, you might be disgusted, you might think he or she is nuts—this is how Pluto teaches you to make up your own mind.

Sure, it's scary to realize that you may have to adjust some of the views that were a comfortable part of your personal world. These emotional security blankets have made you feel safe. However, the more you clutch at them now, the angrier and more unfulfilled you'll feel. The purpose of this transit isn't to randomly destroy your faith but to show you how to re-create it in an honest way.

Breaking the Pattern

Pluto is the portal to that core of inner power most people never use. In the ninth house, you're invited to leap with both feet into your search for the meaning of true humanity.

Keep an open mind. Pluto tears everything apart to find the hidden truths. It may sometimes seem as if everything you've believed in is a lie—and maybe that's true. But it isn't the point. The point is to stop fearing anything that's different.

Listen. Embracing this transit as a chance to learn about other value systems can help you to revise your view of the world without any interference from the self-appointed interpreters of "right" and "wrong."

Learn. Study, read, travel, or talk about cultures, religions, and philosophies different from yours.

Question everything. Don't accept any answer that contains either a threat or an absolute. Whether you're a devout believer, an atheist, or someone who falls between the two, when Pluto moves into your ninth house, you'll begin to question your beliefs. Others will try to sway or threaten or block you from seeking answers outside your world out of fear—but fear prevents change. Enlightenment breaks down the walls of fear and intolerance. And once you break down your own walls, you can help others to find their paths to spiritual freedom too.

PLUTO IN THE TENTH HOUSE

The Phoenix of Integrity

At a Glance: The Tenth House

This is the boardroom that represents the career and public life opposite the fourth house's home and family facade. This house is where we confront issues of ambition, social standards, and the truth between how we act in public and what goes on at home.

The CEO is the dominant parent who either raised the bar, telling us to knuckle down, be diligent, and get straight As, or dropped the ball when setting an example of ethical behavior. This house is where we need to reconcile our private and public lives.

Ethics Check

Pluto is the king of *what goes around comes around*. You can bet your latest sneaky deal that any nasty habits you've refused to acknowledge or embarrassing secrets you've managed to hide are about to go viral.

Whether you're the CEO of a Fortune 100 company or work nine to five in a Dilbert cubicle, having Pluto in your tenth house is like living in a fishbowl. This is the house of public image, located at the top of your natal chart. Think of it this way. It's high noon, you're standing naked in the street, and Pluto's the one who's just ripped off your clothes. He exposes the truth about how you want the world outside to see you and who you really are behind closed doors. When Pluto moves in, the blood bath begins—as if your life is trapped in a sack full of angry cats. This can be one of the toughest transits in the zodiac because Saturn rules the tenth house, and Saturn is Pluto's father—and his archenemy.

Saturn swallowed Pluto and his brother Neptune out of fear of betrayal, as he had betrayed his own father. Ironically, it was this act of prevention that ultimately led to his death—when Jupiter, the one son he failed to eat, forced him to cough up his brothers, and then the three led a rebellion against their father. (Remember the story back in the intro?) When Pluto received Hades, his share of Saturn's estate, he moved underground to guard the gates. He liked it there, and after what he'd been through, he didn't have much use for the outside world.

Saturn's symbolic act of cannibalizing his children represents the smothering you may have received from your father or the authority figure in your childhood. When Pluto marches into your world, his intent is to purge the unhealthy patterns and secrets you may carry. The intention is not to punish you but to release you from the power that swallowed your independence and potential—or worse, the power that has corrupted the sense of integrity you were born with.

Capricorn, the Goat, lives in the tenth house under Saturn's heavy hand. But Capricorn is a determined Earth sign as well as a bossy Cardinal sign. The Goat is diligent and ambitious but has a pessimistic view of life. Instead of rose-colored glasses, Capricorn will often hand you a pair of raincloud-gray ones.

When these three forces rumble, even Darth Vader and his sinister tactics would have a tough time negotiating the territory. "Oh, great," you say? Don't give up and move to a tent in the nearest forest. Pluto is on your side.

Who's the Boss?

If you were born with Pluto in your tenth house, or had this transit during childhood, the themes of ambition, integrity, and authority were played out by your parents. You had your own ideas about what you were going to do with your life and probably felt as if you were destined to do something special. Unless you have achieved your dream, this feeling still circulates through your mind and heart today.

You may have received support from your parents, especially your father or the authority figure in your home. Or your ambitions could have been blocked in any number of ways. Perhaps your parents regarded work as a necessary evil they had to suffer—their focus was inward. A job provided money, and they weren't interested in anything else. Money was simply the trade-off for life's necessities and their ability to do leisure-time activities. Then you come along and want to be president of your own company or country. Or be a doctor, a teacher, or the best investigative journalist in the world. All are big ambitions for a kid. Whatever your dream, they couldn't think beyond hard work and hard knocks. The message you received was, *Life's too short not to enjoy it. Money is only a means to that end.*

Maybe you were a girl who wanted more than high school, marriage, and kids but you were raised to believe, either through generation or culture, that a woman's place was in the home. Even today, the words *women* and *power* used together strike fear into the hearts of traditionalists all over the planet. Your message was, *Don't get above yourself. Find a man instead.*

You could have been a boy whose father equated success with a fat bank account. He may have worked overtime every weekend and/or been a cutthroat businessman who flaunted his wealth. Maybe he'd clawed his way to success from a poor background and wanted to make sure everyone knew he had plenty of cash. What you absorbed: *Only money matters. It doesn't even matter how you make it as long as you have more than anyone you know.* You also subconsciously heard *You're not a real man unless you have a big bankroll.*

Kids with tenth-house Plutos don't want to be just a doctor or a police officer or a veterinarian, they want to be the best and most famous at whatever they do. Sometimes, the negative message comes through kind but misguided efforts to protect them from the harsh realities of trying to succeed. Perhaps your parents shot down your visions with conflicting statements. *Your dreams are wonderful and you're a fabulous kid, but you also have to be realistic. Vet school takes a 4.0 GPA or higher to apply. Even then, the competition is so tough. And police work is dangerous—you might get hurt. A doctor could tell you all about that, they have to see pain and suffering every day.*

Although these types of comments were intended to help you face the real world, the messages you received were that you shouldn't aim too high because you most likely won't succeed. Whatever you wanted was out of reach, too competitive, or too dangerous.

As an adult, you may still carry doubts about your ability, or you may still feel destined for something bigger in life. You may be scrambling to fill your wallet and missing life as a result. Try to remember the childhood message you received and examine your life today in comparison. Are you still living under the shadow of your parents' version of success? What adjustments can you make to get more aligned with your personal ambitions?

Being born with Pluto in your tenth house gives you a direct link to the power within you to still be the best at whatever you want to do. It's never too late to take that power and change the course of your life.

The Price of Ambition

Pluto's crawl through your tenth house can stir up all kinds of subterfuge and career challenges. You might discover that your professional life isn't all you thought it would be when you were clawing your way up the ladder of success. And if you've been less than honest in your climb, Pluto publicizes your double-dealings through a bullhorn. He'll also reveal your blind spots.

Thumping the Bible with one hand and slipping the other under the hem of a believer's skirt? Your pious act is about to get exposed in a floodlight of public humiliation. Hiding your booze bottles in the neighbor's recycling bin at midnight? Prepare to wake up in the gutter to the rumble of the morning's garbage truck.

Perhaps you do get the recognition you want then realize it doesn't mean much. Or you become frustrated because you aren't where you expected to be on your personal success schedule. Pluto's here to give you a reality check. In the tenth house, he demands that you examine the motives that drive your ambition.

Twisting the truth to make yourself look better than you really are? Pluto sees to it that you're caught in the lie—and usually by someone who can't wait to broadcast it to the world. Why do you feel the need to lie in the first place? Are you trying to become more popular? Do you not feel as smart as your peers? Covering up a rough childhood? These are some of the questions you might ask yourself in order to reconcile your inner soul of integrity with the not-so-nice way you may be behaving publicly. This is also what you must do to grow spiritually. If you don't, your carefully embroidered life story will begin to unravel like that of a fallen celebrity who now looks more like the bride of Frankenstein than the dewy-eyed starlet everyone knows and loves on the screen. Welcome to your bona fide Pluto freak-out moment.

Theresa, a once-famous actress, freaked when, after twenty years of cover-ups by her loyal handlers, she found herself the fodder for every gossip rag on the market. When her secrets were exposed and her betrayals revealed, her faux happy family and career fell apart. Frightened and angry, she stubbornly refused to change—at first. Cosmetic surgery and a rehab vacation made her look better, but only she could repair her damaged reputation. Thanks to Pluto, she had to play that part for real. Fortunately for Theresa, she did. After counseling and a lot of hard work, she rewrote her life's script.

Whitney Houston, whose life tragically ended just as she was attempting to restore her reputation and career, had Pluto transiting her tenth house. She was living with the effects of years of drug and alcohol abuse, which all came into harsh focus as she struggled with a damaged voice and failed comeback. The issues she dealt with were classic of a Pluto tenth-house transit.

When Pluto has his claws in your soul, he squeezes until you squeak. In the tenth house, he does it under the spotlight of public opinion. Although your Pluto transit probably won't ever reach the tabloid proportions of a public figure, he doesn't care whether you're an A-list movie star or a hamburger flipper. If something needs fixing between who you are on the inside and how you act on the outside, you must fix it or risk the potentially disastrous results.

Maybe your dilemma is as simple as being frustrated with your current status and realizing it's time to finish school or to apply for a promotion. Or it could be as life altering as deciding to dump a failed relationship or business partnership that's trapped you for too long.

You can accept the challenge or you can keep your head stuck firmly in the sand. Once you accept that you must change, you'll begin to grow. Sure, it's painful. However, you'll stop hiding behind your false facade and start examining your life. The real story might be something you've avoided because of family loyalty, but sacrificing yourself for someone else's dream won't cut it any longer.

Ben was a workaholic. He'd rescued several failed businesses that not only survived but thrived under his guidance, perseverance, and leadership. By every public standard, he was a success. Enter Pluto. Ben began to question his personal values, and as he did, he started to lose clients and money. He'd been the man of the family since he was eighteen, when his dad died, and the message he'd learned was that he must excel in business to provide for his family—even at the expense of his personal dreams.

When Pluto started stirring up his buried feelings, Ben faced the truth. Instead of diving for cover, he said, "You're right. I don't have to run things, beat everyone else's billable hours, and work myself to death." Ben interpreted Pluto's call to action as a reason to rethink his goals, reconnect with his higher power, and be honest with himself about what meant the most to him. He exchanged his image of Wall Street wonder for that of a craftsman who creates beautiful objects made with love—this is what he'd always wanted. He boldly set aside the powerful image he'd carefully cultivated and rediscovered his rich inner resources and personal power.

Ben's story is more amazing because no one in his birth family supported him. They thought he'd lost his mind. Pluto opened his eyes, and Ben realized he could change his life. Unlike aging starlet Theresa, he didn't hide from the truth or make excuses. He took a big risk on himself and gambled everything in order to spend more time with his family and fulfill his dreams. And he turned his creative hobby into a productive business just like he had with the struggling businesses before.

Ben met Pluto's challenge and found Pluto's strength. So can you. You first have to admit you're on the wrong path and be willing to confront the powerful people in your life who want to keep you there. But this doesn't mean starting a fight. When you argue, you're trying to convince someone to agree with you, but it's okay if they don't agree. Just like Ben's family, yours might think you're nuts. Fine, that's their issue. You can't control what anyone else feels or thinks. You can control how you react. Say what you mean in a nonthreatening way. Once you begin to stand up for yourself in a healthy manner, you can rewire your thought patterns and live a more fulfilling life.

Remember, you're naked, and everyone you love, fear, and respect is watching. But Pluto's ready to rumble. If you are, too, you must emotionally and mentally prepare to lose the habits, thought patterns, and lies you grew up with and to which you are still attached. You must be ready to jump when Pluto says jump.

Are you trying to live up to the expectations of your father (or father figure) and hating it? Maybe you come from a long line of successful lawyers or farmers or mechanics. Trouble is that you wanted to be a landscape designer or a writer or an architect. Are you trying to live down your parental figure's bad reputation? Maybe you're embarrassed or ashamed you were poor or don't have a college education. You could be either too competitive or too afraid to compete because of an overbearing father or authority figure. Whatever your truth is, once you admit it, you can begin to work toward the life you want instead of the life that someone else planned for you or that you feel unable to overcome.

Win the Race

After Pluto either shakes you a little or knocks you on your butt, you can expect a chance to get your second wind. No Pluto transit continually slams you into the ground. The effects are more like a steady pressure in one area of your life that builds and releases and builds again. A crisis can burst at either the beginning or the end, but most of the time it's a series of incidents that keep reminding you you're on the wrong course.

Sometimes, your career takes a nosedive. You could get caught in a downsizing or be the victim of underhanded maneuvering by a power player who sees you as a threat. Your business slows to a trickle. Whether you saw it coming or not, you'll experience powerful feelings of anger, shock, fear. Usually, a tenth-house career crash is Pluto's way of telling you that you need to redirect your path. That may not help when the bills are due, and you may have to scramble to find some kind of work that will keep a roof over your head. However, this is a good time to rethink your ambitions. What do you really want to do with your life?

If you're already on that path, chances are you'll find a position that allows you to grow in new and better ways. If you've been slogging through a profession for all the wrong reasons, you now have the freedom to find a career that fits.

Another side of a tenth-house Pluto transit is to teach you when to take—and not be afraid of—the next step up the ladder. The one thing Pluto, Saturn, and Capricorn can agree on is the decision to grab an opportunity that will advance you on your path. Not all of these breaks happen within your career. Maybe you'll decide to volunteer for a cause you've always felt strongly about. But that one act could change your life.

With Pluto in the driver's seat, you'll have to make adjustments. Sometimes, you think you're on the right road and hit a dead end. You lose out on the promotion, or another ugly scene erupts at home. When this happens, Pluto shrugs and tells you to figure out a new way to go. Even then, you may turn around and head in a different direction only to find that you're speeding toward a cliff. *What the hell's going on?*

Pluto may be living in your tenth house, but he isn't here to nurture. He's here to toughen you up. He wants your emotional reflexes to be as sharp as those of a racecar driver dodging traffic on the

track. This transit is about learning how to recognize phony authority figures and maneuver around their power struggles. It's about
recognizing your own career burnout and reshaping your future. It's
also a reality check that exposes the insecurities driving your need
for status and recognition.

Create a New Beginning

Having Pluto in your tenth house is like living with a scandal-sheet
reporter. If you're fresh out of school and ready to conquer the world,
you have the unique opportunity to lay a solid foundation of honesty
and integrity. Just be aware that Pluto will catch every embellishment
in your resume. If you're older and, hopefully, wiser, you get a chance
to revise and readjust to live a more satisfying life. The key to success
is that you tell the truth to yourself first, then to the people in your
world. If you don't, Pluto will. Pluto doesn't give an English farthing
about your sweaty handwringing and panic attacks. The more you
squirm, the harder he hits. If you push back, however, the fear eventually dissipates.

This includes facing the not-so-happy truths about the power
players who shaped you. This can be the father or mother figure you
grew up with or without. It can be a public figure you want to model
your life after, a teacher who inspired or crushed your dreams, or any
bossy person who thought they knew best and you knew nothing. In
the best cases, you make peace. But don't be afraid of a final break.
Both are healing.

Saturn represents every authority figure in your life. Yes, he's
interested in your success and he will help you—if he feels you're
worthy. The price you pay for sticking to someone else's rulebook is
often the loss of your self-confidence, and the loss of it means losing the ability to make decisions that benefit you. You get trapped
in a Saturn-like set of acceptable behaviors and are unable to evolve
because you're either living with or rebelling against someone else's
laws. If you're living them, you end up plodding through life wishing
you were somewhere else. But rebelling can be just as bad. You never

get anywhere, yet you blame anyone but yourself for your trouble. All of these actions have consequences. Pluto sees to that.

He's not concerned with how you feel or the excuses you make. He operates strictly on action and reaction. Hate your boss? You might get fired because she's tired of your attitude. Out to get a rival at work? Maybe he beats you to the punch, steals your cost-savings plan, and gets a bonus for the idea. You can react any way you want to, but you can't expect to get ahead forever when being dishonest. Think about your motives. Is your dislike of your boss really jealousy because you want to move up the ladder? Are you envious of your rival's success?

Once you understand that you're wasting energy in negative actions and emotions, you can break the pattern. Be proactive, not reactive. If you think you're a loser, you will be. If you think you'll never do better, you won't. If you decide you can't overcome your past, you can't.

By being aware of the defense mechanisms you've created to protect yourself, you can begin to build bridges and tear down the walls. You'll learn that there's no need to hide the real you anymore. Besides, it won't do any good.

Can you think of ways to correct what isn't working? Be honest with yourself, and don't be impatient. Pluto's journeys are long and slow for a reason—to give you the opportunity to make positive and permanent change.

Breaking the Pattern

When Pluto barges into your tenth house, he throws the door open to public opinion. You might run for the hammer to nail it shut, but he forces you to look at the perception others have of you in the meantime. If you use the "I can't stand the exposure" excuse, he'll bark, "You can and you will if you want to survive." That's true—you can break with a disastrous past or reconcile an estranged relationship. You can tweak a faltering career or choose an entirely different path. Although Pluto knocks you around with one hand, he holds you up with the other if you're willing to try—especially if you're already on track.

Start by taking a good look at how your public life or career contrasts with your private life. Are you burned out? What would you do if you could earn a living in any way you choose? How balanced are your public and private lives? Most important, are you being true to yourself?

When you follow your own calling, Pluto sees to it that you meet people who support you and that you receive opportunities that highlight your talents. You come full circle to fulfill your dynamic purpose in life and help others who have similar issues to yours.

If you're willing to stay the course while being painfully honest with yourself, you'll discover that it gets easier to recognize the roadblocks and avoid an emotional crash. Capricorn's symbolic Goat is a nimble creature who climbs to the top of his mountain, one sure-footed step at a time. That's how you get to the end of your tenth-house journey.

Change is hard, but nothing is more important than your life and living it in an honest, authentic way. When you reconcile the past and live honestly in the present, your integrity becomes an example that can help to transform the lives of everyone you meet.

PLUTO IN THE ELEVENTH HOUSE

The Phoenix of Revolution

At a Glance: The Eleventh House

Everyone knows your name at the all-night diner. Opposing the fifth house's attention-getting approach to pleasure, eleventh-house dwellers are an eclectic bunch devoted to solving all the problems of the world. Sharing a beer and lots of social intercourse are the types of friendships and support groups we're attracted to.

This is the house of humanity where the soul learns to work for the common good without prejudice.

Strange Encounters

Warning. You're about to become a weirdo magnet. In the eleventh house, Pluto's determined to shake up your social life and test your cringe capacity. Hate rule-breaking nonconformists? Despise white-collar traditionalists? Take off your tunnel-vision blinders, and take a deep breath. When Pluto drops his socks here, it's like entering into group therapy with Dr. Strangelove.

The eleventh house exists to expand your social consciousness. Pluto does it by sending all sorts of freaky people into your life. Creepy? Sometimes. The really scary part is that you'll be attracted to some of them. His purpose is to break down the cultural and personal programming you've been subjected to all your life. If you do, you'll discover that beneath the radical theories, spiked hair, and different lifestyles, just how much alike we humans are.

Pluto's transit of your eleventh house attacks your prejudices. He shatters those preconceived stereotypes and class distinctions, and forces you to examine the motives behind the way you think about other people. During this transit, my-way-or-the-highway egos get bashed.

Although the eleventh house is commonly known as the house of friends, it holds much more than that. Your ideals, goals, and objectives live here too. This house's full name is the Eleventh House of Friends, Groups, and Wishes. And as Pluto does in every transit, he pushes you to not only reach for the future but to release the past. He can help you destroy what's held you back for all the wrong reasons.

Afraid to speak up for yourself? Say hello to a mouthy new pal who believes in telling the brutal truth. Still trapped by the guilt trips your parents laid on you? Meet the free spirit who invites you to a mind-expanding seminar at the local nudist camp. The narrower your view of the world, the more you can expect to run into people whose belief systems are opposed to yours. In the eleventh house, Pluto challenges you to break down the barriers that prevent you from expanding your knowledge and tolerance.

As the saying goes, *it's time to walk the walk*. If your charity work consists of a periodic donation to your favorite cause, Pluto arranges an invitation that allows you to see firsthand what your contributions do by volunteering. Accept. This is your journey to deepen your concern for humanity. Pluto wants you to put faces to that vague term. Whether you're a traditionalist who's suspicious of anyone who doesn't share your buttoned-up views or a radical who believes in unrestrained freedom, during this transit you will have many opportunities to see the other side's point of view.

Your challenge is to evolve beyond the prejudices of your family, social circles, and politics until you realize that most human beings want the same things—peace, safety, and a right to a life free of fear. This is the transit that can help you connect with people who are working for the good of all humankind, not just within and for their groups. But only you can open your eyes.

Disruption, Eruption, and Mayhem

Uranus, the planet of radical change and independence, rules the eleventh house and the rebellious humanitarian sign of Aquarius. Saturn, the planet of tradition and restriction, also influences this area. The last time Pluto shared living space with this bunch was in the turbulent 1960s, when he ignited the voice of social upheaval heard around the world. Uranus breaks rules. Saturn creates them. Pluto ignores them in favor of discovering what works for him.

Uranus was Saturn's father and Pluto's grandfather. Their family saga is full of betrayal, radical upheavals, and death and dismemberment.

To the ancients, Uranus was known as Father Sky. Tellus, his wife, was Mother Earth. Each night he descended, covering Tellus with his blanket of darkness. Though she bore him a dozen children, he didn't like any of them. He threw the youngest six in Tartarus, a dungeon deep within the Earth, below the underworld, which so enraged Tellus that she asked for volunteers among the remaining six children to castrate their father. Saturn accepted the challenge and accomplished it using the flint-edged sickle she had made especially for the task, and the rest of the children were released from the dungeon.

However, as soon as Saturn returned from his treacherous mission, he locked up his siblings again and set himself up as head honcho. Later, when his own children were born, he attempted to wipe them out too, but his plan was foiled, and he was killed by Jupiter, who then freed his brothers Pluto and Neptune. These stories sound familiar because they all deal with repetitive patterns of family dysfunction that even the mythological gods were hard pressed to escape.

Uranus's energy is electrically charged. It hates tradition, and creates mutiny and extreme, sudden surprise. Saturn's energy is power-hungry and controlling. It wants order and conformity—anything outside the norm is unacceptable. Pluto's energy is dark, passionate, and manipulative. It's full of volcanic force but buried deep within the Earth.

When these energies collide, old habits, traditions, and prejudices clash with forward thinking.

The Herd Mentality

Although friendship is a theme of the eleventh house, these aren't the dedicated relationships we see in the seventh house. Aquarius-ruled friends include your volunteer group, your school chums, or the geocaching pals you hang with a couple of nights a week. Other eleventh-house friends are connected to the groups and organizations you belong to—work buddies, your political party, the girls-night-out crowd. These are mostly casual acquaintances. Of course, tight bonds can form, but they aren't the norm, as the eleventh house represents your need for a tribal community outside of your home. When Pluto moves in, he wants you to look at the rest of the world.

Part of your transformation involves making new group connections that change your life in positive ways. The first step is by moving outside your personal comfort zone. Consider attending a few meetings that you would normally avoid. Read about another culture. Take time to get to know a coworker whose lifestyle is different than yours. If you're spiritual, you might visit different kinds of worship services.

Another objective deals with unhealthy friendships and associations. Eliminate them. You have to give up something in order to receive something else—but you don't have to start a war. You can simply begin to distance yourself. Decline the boring lunch. Drop out of a group you've outgrown. People do it all the time. Once you start, new opportunities will appear. Up until now, you've been content to graze with the herd, sharing its grass-high view of life. Knowing you aren't alone can be comforting, however, it can also be stagnating, especially if you've been afraid to speak your mind or to disagree with the group.

If you were born with Pluto in the eleventh house, you are most likely all too familiar with the bigoted or blighted sides of life. Either through your own family, or from the groups you saw or ran around with growing up, you've seen the misery-loves-company archetype played out in various forms. Major themes range from racism, sexism, and homophobia to cults and cultural and/or political hatreds. Lesser ones include clubs, cliques, and causes.

You've seen the bad side of the group's ability to turn into a mob. Maybe you were even a victim. Or you might have been one of the mob. Your family could have told you to stay away from people who weren't your kind. That if they didn't belong in your world, their worlds weren't worth investigating.

Even if you grew up believing this nonsense, you had a deep, natural curiosity about other people. You may have wanted to know how they lived and what they believed because you couldn't lump them into categories as easily as you were supposed to. And you didn't understand what the fuss was about.

But peer pressure is tough to overcome. When you're a kid, an eleventh-house Pluto may be easier to tolerate by going along with the crowd. Unless your family was extremely enlightened, you were probably afraid to cross your groups for fear of being made fun of or worse, being beaten up at recess.

As an adult, you're better armed with life experience to stand apart from the world's bigots, and that's exactly what you are supposed to do. You're the one who can confront their ignorant prejudices and speak the truth.

Dangerous Liaisons

Pluto is a power player. He wants change, but he doesn't want to give up control. You can find yourself feeling exactly the same way. Even if you've been a team player all your life, you may decide that you don't want to follow the leader any longer. This can cause a power struggle—and that's okay. One of the purposes of this transit is to make you conscious of what isn't working and give you the courage to change it for the better.

Remember the schoolyard bully? He lives in the eleventh house. Maybe you were the bully. If so, you're about to suffer karmic kickback from someone even nastier. How about the "in" crowd? They hang out here too. Are you still groveling to be included? Why? Being forced to conform at the risk of being rejected kills your self-esteem. Pluto dares you to take back your power and gives you the backbone to do it if you try.

That courage comes with a warning. He'll also test your motives and ideals. Don't forget that Pluto's scene includes betrayals and deceit. What will you do to get what you want? Do you dog your desire with the single-minded purpose of a celebrity stalker? Are you so obsessed with winning that you resort to lying and cheating to ensure success? He doesn't give a rat's behind whether you get ahead or lose your head. If you're ruthless, you can count on meeting a bigger badass. And if you lie to impress the crowd, you can bet someone will be happy to expose you. Protect yourself by taking an honest look at what motivates your group connections. Being mindful of your true motivations will help you to recognize your behavior patterns within your circle of friends and social networks. Then it's easier to pinpoint the reason behind the behavior.

Pluto is all about intensity. In the eleventh house, he provides plenty of opportunity for extreme encounters. You can get drawn to powerful and persuasive people or factions that want to reform the world. Friendships you make now should have a purpose in your transformation—but be careful. It's as easy to be attracted to a gang of fanatics as it is to a group of humanitarians. Yes, you might want to change your neighborhood, town, or the world. Just don't use strong-arm tactics. Pluto's brass knuckles are bigger than yours.

Speaking of intensity, Pluto's energy is dark, dangerous, and full of sexual undercurrents. Sexual rivalry between you and a pal can erupt. Or you could fall into bed with a friend and just as abruptly decide that wasn't such a good idea. Alternately, a hot affair might fizzle but leave you with a lasting friendship.

Cassie was in tears when she arrived for her consultation. She and Rick, a friend she volunteered with at the local food bank, had stayed late one evening to pack holiday baskets and ended up having sex.

"I don't know how it happened," she said. "One minute we were working and the next, I was coming on to him. At the time, I was overwhelmed with feeling for him. The affair lasted about a week. Now, an uncomfortable distance is growing between us—this is nuts. I care about Rick and don't want to lose our friendship, but he's avoiding me. What can I do?"

It's easy for a shared passion such as Cassie and Rick's commitment to their charity work to boil into physical passion under Pluto's obsessive influence. Both were committed to seeing that every person who needed food would get it, and they worked longer and harder than anyone else to ensure it. Thanks to Pluto in Cassie's eleventh house, it was easy for her admiration and affection for Rick to spiral out of control. She didn't stop to think. Who can in the clothes-ripping moment? The solution was for Cassie to tell Rick exactly how she felt. And when she did, he was relieved, because he felt the same.

Pluto doesn't distinguish between feelings. He churns them all up and leaves the mess for you to sort through. He deals in truth. Sometimes it's painful, but it's always crucial during a Pluto transit. This is your soul test.

People you meet now can also be fanatical, dangerous, or just plain crazy. Maybe your new spiritual leader turns out to be a Kool-Aid-swilling nutcase. Or you could meet a charismatic activist and become obsessed with helping him or her fight for a new cause. You might make friends with a charming person who's really a doomsday prophet with a basement full of military rations and automatic weapons.

Paranoia is one of Pluto's not-so-cheery gifts, and it's crucial that you don't let yourself get overanxious when you run into these types. The eleventh house is about enlightenment. Control freaks who try to keep you in line with guilt, blame, and shame don't belong here. If you find yourself worrying about their destructive BS, you'll know you're on the wrong track. Pluto's purpose is to make you aware of all your options. Your purpose is to choose wisely. Besides, there's a little sinner in every saint. Embracing yours while understanding that it doesn't have to control your life will keep you balanced.

People you meet during this transit can become powerful allies who open doors for you in amazing ways. Maybe you run into a nice woman at a political rally and she happens to be the CEO of a firm you've just applied to for a job. Perhaps you're a struggling artist and, by chance, meet the owner of a gallery who is willing to look at your work. With Pluto in your eleventh house, either by birth or through transit, you'll often see a burst of success that you owe to someone you meet on a casual basis.

Nowhere to Hide

There's a duality to Pluto's visit to the eleventh house. He's still a loner who likes solitude, and he couldn't care less about group consensus or majority rule. The paradox is that, if you're a loner too, he will shove a variety of new people in your face. Hey, he doesn't have to change, you do. Sometimes, a need for solitude can morph into a fear of any social contact during this trip because of the wide variety of new people tramping through your life. But you don't want to become the hoarder next door who lives under piles of junk, too afraid to live out in the world.

Everyone feels like pulling the covers over their heads now and then. However, if you find yourself pulling away from your friends or getting anxious when you're in a group, then you need to search for the cause. Maybe a friend dumped you in the past and something has triggered that memory. Perhaps a family member or a parent either emotionally or physically left you. Don't let Pluto paranoia invade your head. Reach out to someone you trust for reassurance.

So what if sometimes you feel like just staying home? Do it. Even if your calendar is crammed, you'll most likely have times when you feel the urge to be alone. Everyone needs the occasional breather. When you're operating from the positive side of your transformation, these periods of solitude are healthy ways to stay spiritually and emotionally balanced.

Intense relationships can blow up too easily under Pluto's pressure-cooker influence, so you should gauge your progress by contemplating why you're avoiding the social scene. Feelings of panic and anxiety are destructive. If you have them, it's time to talk to a friend. And if they continue to linger, consider consulting a professional.

In addition to exacerbating your fears, Pluto in the eleventh house also shovels up your past bad behaviors. Think you know all the answers? An idea you hatched could get vetoed by the group. Always been the boss of your gang? Your victims could wise up and leave you without a fan club. If you're wondering why you're being banished from the guest list and everyone's turning their backs on you, it's time to take a serious look at your behavior. On the other hand, if you've been working for positive change in your life, you'll get the opportunity to meet new people who share your interests.

Join In

Not all Pluto transits are alike. Maybe you just need a basic lesson in how to be friends without being possessive. Fortunately, eleventh-house friendships are close but more casual, so experiment with new relationships. Uranus is king of *aha* moments. Be brave. Have dinner with a card-carrying activist. Go to an offbeat for you club. Excluding all the other interesting people you meet puts you at a distinct disadvantage. Even if you don't feel the need to change your current social structure, you should try to embrace new concepts.

The off switch in this enlightenment lamp is that Pluto cringes at happy chatter and meaningless small talk. Like his father, Saturn, he hates it when too many people have too good a time. You just want to have fun, and he tosses a serious issue in your face. You ignore it and keep dancing. He counters with a revelation that one of your buddies is spreading rumors about you. You vow to get even, and he just escalates the fight until your other friends dump you both. Confront your betrayer in private. Whether you end the friendship or forgive her is your choice. However, while you're thinking about it, consider what you might have done to contribute to the jealousy or anger that inspired her attempt to discredit you.

Pluto makes you confront what he considers your superficial connections. Are you going to sign up for dance lessons again? Do you want to stick with the bowling league another season? Is it okay to keep some of the old networks? Sure. As always, balance is the key. Keep the connections that work and dump the ones that don't. Just be sure to stay open to new relationships.

Part of your eleventh-house lesson is learning to detach. You might be attracted to a new friend and want to hang out all the time, but she's a social butterfly. If you've been possessive of these types of relationships in the past, the lesson will be harder to learn. If you don't learn it, you'll keep knocking your head against the doors of people who don't want to hear you ringing the bell every five minutes. That's Pluto's control-freak energy at work.

On the other hand, if you've closed yourself off from forming casual relationships, you could find that you're the adored object of obsessive people. That's why you may discover that you're battling for control of your social circle, being smothered by a new friend, or attracting destructive people. You may have the reputation of collecting stray people like some people rescue abandoned puppies. Although both are noble thoughts, when the creatures threaten to take over your life, you need to cull the herd before you lose your mind.

Breaking the Pattern

Pluto moves into the eleventh house to awaken your social conscience. Freedom of self-expression for every human is a key trait of this abode. So is tolerance and broad-mindedness. When Pluto arrives, he begins to shatter your preconceived attitudes and prejudices.

Pluto's move-in with Uranus recharges your mental batteries. He shows you how to trust your intuition while letting the skeptics, fanatics, and lunatics stay in the dark if they choose. Your soul is meant to focus on the bigger social issues, which, when distilled, means speaking out against bigotry wherever you find it—including within your own tribe.

A good way to begin this journey is with silence. Sometimes, refusing to laugh at a demeaning joke or clichéd comment is louder than voicing a protest. This approach can reduce any fears you might have about contradicting the crowd.

Breaking away from a negative group paves the way for Pluto to send new people into your life who share your beliefs. You can do this by just dropping out or gradually detaching yourself. When you're asked why you aren't around as much, you must be honest. You don't have to argue, but you do have to state the reason you're going.

When you rise to the challenges of this transit, you learn to appreciate the value of the differences in people. You let go of stereotypes. When you begin to see humanity as individuals who strive for the same freedoms as you—and become part of that process—you begin to transform. That's when you lose the fear of speaking against prejudice and can stand up for every person everywhere—including you.

PLUTO IN THE TWELFTH HOUSE

The Phoenix of Acceptance

At a Glance: The Twelfth House

Finally, we arrive in the attic. The twelfth house holds our secrets, illusion, and the subconscious. The hidden emotions we've stashed up here influence all aspects of our lives. This is the house of mystery and mayhem where we've piled every hurt and emotional injury.

The riches stored in this scene include empathy, sympathy, and an instinctive understanding of life. This house holds the key to the soul's evolution into spiritual and emotional healing.

Unlock Your Prison

In the twelfth house, Pluto, the lord of brutal truth, meets Neptune, the king of deception. The pits in this boneyard are full of denial and surrounded by a wall of passivity. Nothing's tougher or trickier to smash.

When Pluto unlocks the creaky door of your private prison in the tower, you step into a familiar space cluttered with every piece of mental garbage you've collected throughout your life. All of them trigger the shoot-your-foot reactions that interfere with your success, all push your guilt button, and all wield a powerful but unconscious influence on your life. If your palms start to sweat as long-gone issues pop into your head, you're starting to feel the pressure of navigating this maze of truth and lies.

The good news? On the other side of the room are the creative, intuitive, and visionary energies of the twelfth house. However, you can't reach these transformative qualities until you haul out your emotional trash. Step carefully. The floor in the twelfth house is mined with self-sabotaging traps. And in case you're in a fog about what they look like, when Pluto appears, he blows a few up in your face as a reminder.

Of all of Pluto's transits, this is the most complex and contradictory. There's usually no room to distort the truth with Pluto, yet the truth is always distorted in the twelfth house because illusion-loving Neptune rules the place. Feel crazy yet? Give yourself time.

Pluto is a power player. He wants control and often manipulates the scenario to ensure that he wins. He's also Neptune's brother, and both rule the Earth's hidden realms—Pluto lives underground in Hades, Neptune resides in the murky depths of the sea. And these two were playing head games millennia before the Kardashians decided to televise their family drama.

Pisces, the sign of compassion, empathy, and avoidance also lives here. The Fishes that symbolize this Mutable-Water sign are eternally tied together but seem to swim in opposite directions. But their standard wallow-in-misery-or-reach-for-the-stars description is a misconception. Any sign that called this emotion-packed place home would have some miserable days. However, Pisces's duality isn't as simplistic as *sink or swim*. The Fishes represent the ability to connect the spiritual and physical worlds. Pisces is intuitive and can sense the emotional undercurrents that swirl around them, sometimes overwhelming them.

Most of us have walked into a roomful of people at one time or another and picked up the current of emotion running through the air. If you were born with or have Pluto transiting your twelfth house, you may unconsciously absorb this energy far more often and not know why you feel sad or tired, or get the jitters. Maybe you pick up the anger shimmering off the woman in front of you at the checkout counter. Or you shiver with unease when a man brushes past you in a crowd. This spiritual antenna picks up waves of energy from other people like your favorite music station picks up radio signals.

When you combine all these traits, it's easy to see why the twelfth house can be last on the zodiac's list of favorite places to flop. Sure, it's full of escapism and self-delusion; it also holds compassion and acceptance and peace. And those are the gifts that Pluto's here to help you reach.

Subtle Sabotage

The twelfth house is also known as the house of secret enemies. However, this isn't the whole story. Sure, you might discover that a friend has been talking trash behind your back, but you think you're innocent. What's closer to the truth is that your actions are coming back to haunt you. Maybe your pal's found out about the closet affair you had with his guy last year. Or perhaps you have to admit a humiliating truth about yourself.

When he was in his early twenties, Bryan worked as a cashier at a family-owned business one summer. The job paid minimum wage, and though he worked overtime whenever possible, he'd run out of money two or three days before his paycheck came. The first few times Bryan borrowed from the petty-cash box, he paid it back. Soon, supplementing his income became a habit. Eventually, so did forgetting to replace the money.

During the next twenty years, Bryan forgot his petty crime. However, he continued to cheat his employers by getting paid for overtime he didn't work. He helped himself to his friends' food or booze without contributing his share. He borrowed cars and left the gas tanks empty. He didn't rob banks or become a break-in artist, but stealing became the theme of Bryan's life.

When he opened a small business, he drove himself crazy because he didn't trust his employees. He was intolerant of the most minor rule-breaking, and fired anyone he even suspected of dishonesty. His employee turnover rate was so high that it affected his profits, but Bryan hadn't made the connection between his dishonesty and his distrust of everyone else. Instead, he stuffed that dark trait deep inside his personal dungeon.

Then Pluto arrived in the form of a former friend he hadn't seen in ten years. Over lunch, which Bryan paid for, the friend joked that was the first time he'd ever seen Bryan pick up the check, adding that he was happy to see that Bryan had left his "flaky days" behind. When Bryan questioned him, the friend related more stories about the way Bryan took advantage of everyone he knew.

"I was numb," he said. "That night, at home, I thought about what Peter had said. I realized I had been a flake, and I took what I wanted without a second thought. I remembered stealing from the couple who hired me when I was a kid. They never mentioned it, so I told myself that they didn't care about a couple of bucks a week."

Pluto is neutral. He doesn't judge and he doesn't worry. He brings about change by showing you the truth. Whether you change or not—and whether that change is positive or negative—is up to you. After Bryan's revelation, he began to treat his employees better. He relaxed the rules and behaved as if he trusted instead of suspected them. As a result, his profits are up and his turnover rate is almost zero. Pluto made him see an unpleasant fact about himself that affected the way he treated others, and Bryan conquered it.

The twelfth house contains secrets you think are buried and the shameful memories you've distorted into justifiable actions. Pluto will point them out, but it's still your job to separate fact from fantasy.

Compassion Begins at Home

Another twelfth-house topic is the gift of bringing healing energy to others. Pluto's transit gives you a special opportunity to become a source of compassion for anyone who needs a kind word or touch. And the first person in line should be *you*.

The twelfth house holds the answers to both acceptance and self-destruction. Pluto boosts the power of your memory and shoots you a hefty dose of paranoia. You become ultrasensitive to a look or a word. The slightest argument triggers a flood of *poor me* emotions. You not only fixate on every unkind word and action of the moment, you flash back to similar events in the past then examine them both under the microscope of self-pity.

While you're trying to process all of that, Pluto dredges up another unpleasant scene from your past. You seethe with anger. He picks his teeth and tosses in yet another new glitch. Perhaps you meet a modern copy of an old tormentor. Will you walk into the ego crusher again? If you do, will you beat yourself up with guilt over being stupid or naïve to suffer the same wound again?

Do you finally recognize the pattern? Until you do, you'll see Pluto winding up again and again to pitch more self-esteem crushing tests at you.

Traditional twelfth-house contents include mental or physical suffering, hidden enemies, the unconscious, and any places of confinement such as jails, asylums, and hospitals. If you were born with Pluto in your twelfth house, your home life could have been shadowed by one of these influences. Maybe your father was a drunk who spent the milk money on booze. Or one of your parents might have had a chronic illness and the shadow of that hung over your family. Because this house is so psychically attuned, the hurt you suffered doesn't have to be a personal one. You were born connected to the pain and suffering of others. Either way, your natural self-defense mechanism would be to avoid the pain by burying it.

To evolve, you must accept the fact that the pain happened. This transit isn't as simple as *forgive and forget*—although you might do one or both, or neither. Acceptance is neither forgiveness nor forgetfulness. It's simply acknowledging that the hurt happened. Dad went to jail for drunk driving, Mom was ill all the time, and you couldn't have helped either of them. Focusing on the truth without replaying the anger or guilt helps you heal. Picking at the wound only prevents you from moving forward.

Another key to surviving Pluto's harsher aspects is to stop judging yourself and others. Neptune has no boundaries. Your need to continually damn the people who hurt you or to punish yourself for the hurt you've caused others will also know no boundaries unless you quit rerunning the list of accusations through your head. Judgment contains anger, sorrow, fear, victimization—all the self-sabotaging land mines that blow up and stop you from reaching the gifts your twelfth house contains.

Sometimes people say that they know God has forgiven them but they can't forgive themselves. Eternal martyrdom is self-serving. Worse, it might be the height of hubris.

If you are truly ready to heal, you can discover the inner strength you need to stand up to any traumas you may have suppressed. Pluto reminds you that, until you make this conscious choice and accept the truth—the past—without judgment, nothing will change, and you cannot evolve.

Save-the-World Syndrome

Neptune is idealistic and Pisces is a dreamer. Add Pluto's fanaticism and you could get carried away with a vision of saving the world. What's wrong with that? Nothing, as long as you control your ego. Pluto causes power struggles wherever he goes, and one of the biggest fights occurs here, in his brother Neptune's house.

Following someone who insists he or she has all the answers is a dangerous illusion that sets you up to be victimized. If you haven't realized the truth about these types of fanatics, you could get trapped by their unhealthy beliefs. You could also turn into a lesser version of the all-knowing visionary and try to force your ideas onto anyone who'll hang around and listen.

Keeping a healthy distance from any source of radical thinking can be difficult, especially in today's socially connected world. With Pluto nearby, keeping yourself safe from being sucked into that mindset is easier. A little humility and a genuine desire to serve others without being self-serving can protect you.

Whatever your age, a twelfth-house transit teaches you how to blend reflection with action. You're challenged to connect with your higher power. These are the years when you can conquer your self-defeating behaviors by releasing anger and fear, and learning the healing power of acceptance without judgment.

Time Out

One of the traits Neptune bestows is the need for solitude. Pisces, the sign that occupies the twelfth house, is known for periodic retreats from the world. Your lesson may be to learn how to balance your physical, emotional, and spiritual needs. When Pluto arrives, you begin to feel the pressure to slow down.

If you're a hard-driving type, this transit can signal a warning to stop abusing your body and/or your mind. Working sixty-hour weeks? Running to keep up with your partying buddies? Because Pluto understands that most humans learn the hard way, he's fully prepared to turn up the heat until you boil in your own excesses. Your 24/7 lifestyle will turn to burnout, your physical or emotional self-abuse will become a flameout, and your denial will land you in the hospital or the nearest shrink's office.

Mike never had a spare moment. Between work, children, volunteer events, the gym, and the active social life he shared with his wife, he barely had time to sleep. And on those rare days when he was free of obligations, he'd pace around the house until he found a minor repair to tackle, or he'd head outside and work in the yard. Relaxation wasn't only something he didn't do, the idea of lying in the sun, sitting quietly with a book, or just vegging out on the couch was as foreign as the thought of retiring—ever.

The first jolt of Mike's Pluto visit came at his annual physical, when his doctor told him his blood pressure was a little too high. Mike said he'd been under extra pressure at work, but the busy season would end soon and then he could get some sleep. He balked at the idea of taking prehypertension medication, so the doctor agreed to check him again in three months.

The Pluto alarm rang a few weeks later when he became dizzy and tight chested on his morning run before breakfast. But, as always, he pushed himself to perform. When he got home, he was pale and sweating. Mike's wife made him sit down as she called the doctor, who told them to get to the ER.

Mike was lucky. Although he suffered a mild heart attack, he could have just as easily dropped dead. His years of nonstop commotion had stopped him cold.

The Pluto transit in this case activated the theme of solitude as a means of spiritual renewal. Mike was too busy for meditation or self-reflection, or even a nap on a Sunday afternoon. So Pluto gave him some time to think. Today, Mike's healthy and has finally learned the value of quiet time.

Neptune and Pisces deal with the inner world, and when they connect with Pluto, your inner world gets an overhaul. You don't have to trek to Tibet on a spiritual quest (although, under this influence, you might). However, you do need to slow your pace and enjoy your life more. If this cycle comes in later life, for example, you might decide to retire early. Whatever your age, the message is that quiet time is as crucial to your well-being as any physical challenge or career success.

Reflect on the motion versus the commotion in your life. Are you running in circles and missing life's pleasures? Do you feel guilty about taking time for yourself? Think about how you can carve some solitude out of your week.

Breaking the Pattern

This is the transit of getting in touch with the compassion within your soul, and recognizing that you are truly a spiritual being.

In order to reach your inner light, you have to trek through the darker traits you've buried in your subconscious, such as the wounds you've suffered and those you've inflicted on both yourself and others. Pluto's churning through your subconscious will certainly drain your energy as he forces you to deal with these painful memories and overcome the trap of self-sabotage, but the end result will be well worth the journey. Here's what to do:

Accept your life as it's happened. The point of this transit is to show you that you aren't here to suffer. And that acceptance is not forgiveness. It's acknowledging the hurts you've endured instead of holding them inside, where they gnaw at your soul.

Show compassion to yourself and to others. The act of compassion is neither judgmental nor pitying. It's a deep understanding of the human need for unconditional love.

Become a visionary. Share your ideals and put your words into actions. Act with humility, not ego.

Release guilt. Punishing yourself for what you've done to others or to yourself, or for what you were unable to prevent from happening to you or to someone you loved, does nothing but continue your cycle of pain. If you need to apologize to someone, do it. If that person is you, tell yourself you're sorry.

Relax. The mind–body–spirit balance is crucial to connecting with your higher power. Find your solitude, and make it a fundamental part of your life.

During this transit you are being asked to clean out your mind's attic-prison of emotional clutter so that you can tune in to the spiritual side of your being. When you do, you will become one of the lights of compassion that shines through the darkness in the world.

CONCLUSION

Conquering Your World with Pluto

Whether we like it or not, Pluto always has the upper hand. And he won't go away until he teaches us what we need to know. Although he can be a grim guy, he's also the god of buried wealth—wealth he's willing to share. But you have to pay attention to the signals he sends, just like you'd pay attention to the path drawn on a treasure map.

Think of Pluto's energy as a series of cosmic wakeup calls. The first is subtle like a firm hand quietly nudging you. You're annoyed and try to shake it off, but it returns like a drunken ex who keeps calling after the bars close. The second sounds like the insistent buzz of your alarm—except when Pluto's buzzing, the noise steadily increases until you feel as if your head's caught in a wood chipper. The third cuts to the chase with a bomb blast to your psyche. Depending on where you are in your personal journey with Pluto, you could receive one or all.

Ready to dive under the bed? Hang on a second. Working through your Pluto issues isn't easy, but it isn't impossible either. You already have the power to succeed within you. And here are ten tips for traveling with Pluto and living to tell the tale:

1. **Be mindful.** Most days, we walk around on autopilot. Being aware of what you say and do begins the process of change. Here's a suggestion—start by eliminating the word *fine* from your vocabulary, and see where that small change takes you.

2. **Grow a backbone.** Digging into the deepest part of yourself takes guts. It may also take therapy and perhaps a drink or two.

However, Pluto's transit isn't all destruction and mayhem. Most of the time, it's a steady pressure that attempts to make you conscious of what's no longer working in your life. Facing it can be frightening, but ignoring it can lead to disaster.

3. **Be honest.** Admit your part in your problems. Once you do, it's easier to stop attracting the same negative situations. Of course, you don't have to publically confess either. This should be an inward journey, not reality TV.

4. **Take control.** *No* is a powerful word. Use it when you really mean it and you'll start simplifying your life in amazing ways.

5. **Forgive yourself.** Using your guilt against you is a manipulator's favorite weapon. When you refuse to step into passive-aggressive land with an emotional blackmailer (including yourself), give yourself twenty Pluto points.

6. **Forgive your bullies.** Revenge may taste sweet, but it's self-defeating to hang on to a grudge. While you're wallowing in hatred, that jerk you despise is out having fun somewhere.

7. **Ditch your inner victim.** What's the opposite side of the hubris coin? Self-effacement taken to the level of self-destruction. During a Pluto transit, you'll find more than one person who wants to crucify you. Don't hand them the hammer and nails.

8. **Work that body.** Pluto's sometimes-stressful energy isn't easy to endure, but exercise is a great emotional release. So is sex, a totally Pluto activity.

9. **Chill.** As scary as Pluto can be, his mission is to help you purge the ghosts of the past and live a true-to-you life. Don't feed your fears by imagining the worst-case scenario. Pluto transits can be decades long which gives you plenty of time to make permanent changes.

10. **Be open.** Pluto's the universe's hard case, but if you want to change, he'll show you how. Forget the pep talks—you don't even have to believe in yourself at first. You just have to do the work. With each step forward, you'll become stronger.

So, now that you've learned some of the ways in which Pluto can bolster or blast your life, what are you going to do with this information?

Pluto affects us in many ways—primarily, by testing us to see if we're paying attention to our lives. Unless you start noticing your habits and being mindful of the choices you make, nothing's going to change. Believe us, we've seen this hundreds of times, and we've lived it in our own lives.

What no longer serves you? This simple question is multilayered and deceptive, its answers can be as straightforward as a broken appliance you need to replace or as complex as a self-defeating behavior pattern that prevents your success. It could even be your own attitude that keeps you from spiritually moving forward.

Without taking responsibility for your life, change won't happen. And it's a slow process. Through astrology, you can learn what your auto-responses are. Learn how Pluto works throughout your life to see the patterns you choose. Become mindful of what you do so you can change those auto-responses into thoughtful and meaningful replies. This doesn't mean you walk around in a Zen state of mind, with a permanent angelic smile slapped on your face. It means that when you're angry, you don't automatically reach for food or booze or the nearest credit card. It also means that you stop recycling through the hurt locker of relationships.

Facing our demons and believing that we can conquer them is not easy—you know that. What we want you to understand is that you hold the power to change your life. We've given you some guidelines and shown you how astrology can help, but you have to do the work. You'll also get the reward. And no one can ever take that away from you.

ACKNOWLEDGMENTS

Thank you, Fridays—John Brantingham, Dennis Caeton, Dennis Lewis, and Kathleen Puckett.

—Hazel Dixon-Cooper

Thanks to my dear friends who staunchly urged me to continue throughout the Sturm und Drang of health problems, keeping my mega site going, and smiling more than crying: published writer and close friend Valerie Beth Gilbert; and my best friends Bonnie Hutton, Nancy Oliver, Holly Gleason, and Jodi Wells. I also wish to acknowledge the support and courage of Terrence McKee, Beth Rifkin, Debra D. Allen, Dalia Koss, and Ineta McParland, who lovingly keep me on track. Thanks also, to my sweet friend Richie Sambora, who's my biggest motivator; Cher, who said, "Bridge, it's time"; and Paulette Howell, who's been my confidante for years.

—Bridgett Walther

RESOURCES AND RECOMMENDED READING

Websites

Hazel Dixon-Cooper's website: hazeldixoncooper.com
Bridgett Walther's website: bridgettwalther.com
www.crystalinks.com/romegods.html
www.ancientgreece.com/s/Mythology
www.theoi.com

Books

Archetypes of the Zodiac, by Kathleen Burt (Llewellyn Publications, 1999)

Planets in Transit, by Robert Hand (Para Research, 1976)

The Only Astrology Book You'll Ever Need, by Joanna Martine Woolfolk (Revised edition, Taylor Trade Publishing, 2012)

Who's Who in Classical Mythology, by Michael Grant and John Hazel (Oxford University Press, 1993)

Books by the Authors

Hazel Dixon-Cooper
Born on a Rotten Day (Fireside / Simon & Schuster, 2002)
Friends on a Rotten Day (Red Wheel / Weiser Books, 2007)
Love on a Rotten Day (Fireside / Simon & Schuster, 2004)
Work on a Rotten Day (GPP Life / Global Pequot Press, 2010)

Bridgett Walther
Conquer the Cosmos (Plume/Penguin, 2010)

QUICK GUIDE TO ROMAN GODS AND OTHER MYTHOLOGICAL PEOPLE AND CREATURES

ROMAN NAME	GREEK NAME
Alcmene (mortal)	Alcmene
Apollo	Apollo
Cancer (the Crab; monster)	Carcinus/Karkinos
Castor (mortal)	Castor
Ceres	Demeter
Chiron	Chiron
Cupid	Eros
Daphne	Daphne
Diana	Artemis
Europa	Europa
Eurystheus	Eurystheus
Faunus	Pan
Ganymede	Ganymede
Hercules	Heracules
Hydra (monster)	Hydra
Juno	Hera
Jupiter	Zeus
Justitia	Astraea
Juventas	Hebe

ROMAN NAME	GREEK NAME
Ladon	Ladon
Leda (mortal)	Leda
Mars	Ares
Mercury	Hermes
Nemean Lion	Nemean Lion
Neptune	Poseidon
Ops	Rhea
Orion (mortal)	Orion
Penelope	Penelope
Pholus	Pholus
Pluto	Hades
Pollux	Pollux
Proserpina	Persephone
Saturn	Cronus
Tellus	Gaia
Tyndareus (mortal)	Tyndareus
Typhon (monster)	Typhon
Ulysses	Odysseus
Uranus	Ouranos/Uranus
Venus	Aphrodite

GLOSSARY

Air: The Element associated with intellect, communication, curiosity, attitude, and thinking. The three Air signs are Gemini, Libra, and Aquarius. (See also *Earth*, *Fire*, and *Water*.)

Ascendant (rising sign): The constellation that is rising over the horizon at the time of birth, and located in the First House of Self. The degree of the Ascendant indicates the exact moment of birth and is associated with the pattern of outward action/reaction, first impressions, and mannerisms—one's personality. It is also looked at for clues to health issues. (See also *Sun sign*.)

Cardinal: The Quality/Modality associated with initiating action and managing others. These personalities are linked with change and new beginnings. Each season of the year begins with a Cardinal sign. The Cardinal signs are Aries, Cancer, Libra, and Capricorn. (See also *Fixed* and *Mutable*.)

Earth: The Element associated with stability, grounding, loyalty, and possessiveness. The three Earth signs are Taurus, Virgo, and Capricorn. (See also *Air*, *Fire*, and *Water*.)

Elements: The basic essences for life as defined by Western astrology. The Elements (in the order they appear on the zodiac wheel) are Fire, Earth, Air, and Water.

Feminine: The receptive Polarity associated with strong inner reserves and sensitivity. Opposite of Masculine. The Feminine Sun signs are Taurus, Cancer, Virgo, Scorpio, Capricorn, and Pisces. (See also *Masculine* and *Polarity*.)

Fire: The Element associated with enthusiasm, inspiration, self-confidence, and impulsiveness. The three Fire signs are Aries, Leo, and Sagittarius. (See also *Air*, *Earth*, and *Water*.)

Fixed: The Quality/Modality of stability, perseverance, personal magnetism, resourcefulness, and loyalty. The Fixed signs are Taurus, Leo, Scorpio, and Aquarius. These personalities can be rigid and slow to change. (See also *Cardinal* and *Mutable*.)

Houses: Division of the horoscope into twelve segments beginning with the Ascendant (First House). Each house represents an area of life and corresponds to specific functions and issues of daily living.

Masculine: The assertive Polarity associated with action and sociability. Opposite of Feminine. The Masculine Sun signs are Aries, Gemini, Leo, Libra, Sagittarius, and Aquarius. (See also *Feminine* and *Polarity*.)

Modalities: See *Qualities*.

Mutable: The Quality/Modality associated with the flexible/adaptable energy that gives one the ability to compromise. Too much Mutable energy results in a scattered personality that rarely finishes anything it starts. (See also *Cardinal* and *Fixed*.)

Natal chart: An astrology chart that provides a snapshot of the placements of the zodiac signs and houses at the exact moment of birth. Also called the birth chart. Its purpose is to gain insight into a person's character, potential, strengths, and challenges.

Polarity: The division of signs into Masculine (direct) and Feminine (receptive) opposition. The oppositions are Aries-Libra, Taurus-Scorpio, Gemini-Sagittarius, Cancer-Capricorn, Leo-Aquarius, and Virgo-Pisces. (See also *Feminine* and *Masculine*.)

Qualities: Also known as the Modalities, these are the three types of energies that govern action and reaction. They are Cardinal, Fixed, and Mutable.

Rising sign: See *Ascendant.*

Ruling planet (or ruler): The planet associated with the ego and unconscious drives of a sign, as its traits function strongly in the sign. The ruling planet is said to be "at home" in the sign.

Sun sign (or zodiac sign): The sign of the zodiac in which the Sun is located at any given time. The Sun sign determines one's inner character (whereas the Ascendant determines the outward personality). (See also *Ascendant.*)

Symbols: The zodiac symbol represents the essence of the Sun sign, and the Sun sign is said to have the traits of it symbol (usually an animal or other living creature). See the Quick Guide to the Zodiac Houses and Pluto's Influence table on pages 79–80 for a complete listing of the symbols, including their signs and houses.

Transit: The movement of a planet through a sign of the zodiac, and a means of predicting events.

Trine(d): The most harmonious aspect (relationship) between the Sun signs or planets. A trine brings advantages through ease of communication and a natural understanding. Sun signs sharing the same Elements are trined. Fire signs Aries, Leo, and Sagittarius. Earth signs Taurus, Virgo, and Capricorn. Air signs Gemini, Libra, and Aquarius. Water signs Cancer, Scorpio, and Pisces.

Water: The Element associated with emotion, empathy, psychic intuition, and nurturing. The Water signs are Cancer, Scorpio, and Pisces. (See also *Air, Earth,* and *Fire.*)

Zodiac sign: See *Sun sign.* (See also *Ascendant.*)

ABOUT THE AUTHORS

Hazel Dixon-Cooper has been a professional astrologer for more than twenty-five years. She is the author of the bestselling Rotten Day humorous astrology book series and has written astrology articles and columns for a variety of newspapers and magazines, including *Cosmopolitan*'s Bedside Astrologer column for eight years. She is a popular guest on a wide variety of international, national, and regional radio programs.

Bridgett Walther has been a professional astrologer for more than thirty-five years. She has written astrology, advice, and numerology columns for a variety of publications such as *Elle* magazine, *Life & Style*, Playboy.com, and WomansDay.com. She's been a guest astrologer for the *CBS Morning Show*, the drive-time astrologer for the Chicago Radio Syndicate, and is the author of *Conquer the Cosmos*. Her extensive client list includes celebrities such as Cher, Heather Locklear, Richie Sambora, and Chazz Palminteri.